Essentials of Litigation

Things You Encounter
On the Way to Court

First Print Edition, 2014

N. Madera Aguilar

To All Litigants

Table of Contents

Part One

Your Way to Court

AUTHOR'S NOTE

This is one of the author's works on legally-related subjects with the Philippine setting as the foreground.

Jurisprudence in the Philippine context is a rich source of wisdom, guidelines, precepts and reference which a citizen may avail of in application to his courses of action as well as routine activities making up his daily chores. The provisions of the Rules of Court, which govern law practice and procedural undertakings in judicial fora, find amplification in decisions, resolutions and rulings which the highest court of the land, the Supreme Court, hand down as a result of evaluation, consideration and deliberation on questions brought before it.

The author thus finds it a rare privilege to be able to share to the rest of the world the product of his research utilizing the available data in reliance to the foregoing. On their way to court, litigants or laymen may find a perfect answer to a concern brought forth, or it may be otherwise, a realization of an outcome which may be unexpected.

Through this work, the author envisions that at least, or in whatever small means, one who proceeds on his way thereto may have an inkling of what is being tackled there.

As will be stated in the foreword herein, reference to a particular rule in the Rules of Court aforementioned is by its number and in jurisprudence by a case record number as well as the date of promulgation. This provides the facility if browsing upon the entire issuance is desired. Resort to condensation, abbreviation and capsulation is inevitable to meet printing and formatting needs as well as the niceties of publishing and coming out with the E-Book version of this work.

The author makes known his gratitude to all those who have afforded his works their patronage.

FOREWORD

"On the way to court" as used in this volume should be understood as the status of one who is preparing for litigation. There are various reasons why we seek the intervention of courts and it is significant for a layman to have at least a capsular view of what usually takes place therein. Although the ramifications dished out in this book are primarily based on the Philippine usage and experience, it has to be borne in mind that the tenets and precepts adhered to are almost uniform in their global application. The same practices hold true: that there is a seeker of recourse and there is someone from whom it is sought. For a plaintiff there is a defendant. For a petitioner there is a respondent. For a complainant there is an accused.

It is thus in the light of the foregoing that the rules and jurisprudence maintained in the Philippine setting are used as basis for this book. As to citations in the work, a *GR number* refers to the identification of the record in the set of cases decided by the Supreme Court, the highest tribunal in the judicial hierarchy of the country, with the appurtenant date when the same was promulgated. The Rule cited refers to the Revised Rules on Civil Procedure presently being in effect and the number cited refers to a particular rule from where the provision was sourced and lifted as a passage.

The author trusts that whatever little input he invested in this book will go along way towards achieving the goal of global sharing, especially to the laymen, of invaluable information from the point of view of the Philippine legal system.

This book, however, should be availed of merely from its academic standpoint and must not to be treated as a substitute for seeking professional advice from practitioners whose expertise will have to be sought for by those who may need the same in the applicable legal perspective.

Chapter 1
Going to Court

Litigation is not easy. It entails a lot of hassle and technicalities. One resorts thereto to enforce a right, insist on a claim, vindicate one's pride or defend a cause. One goes to court in order that he can have his day therein.

You go to court by suing someone, in which case you shall be the plaintiff. If you are the one being sued you become the defendant. This is true in a civil case. But in a criminal action, it is the state or the people who are deemed the plaintiff and if you are the defendant or respondent you become the accused. The private complainant is considered merely as a complaining witness.

To start with, you hire the services of counsel to represent you in court in a civil case. In a criminal case, it is the state prosecutor who takes up the cudgels for you as he is actually lawyering for the state or the people. In either case, the defendant or accused is counseled by a private lawyer or in the case of an accused who cannot afford the services of a private counsel (counsel *de parte*) he is given a counsel *de officio* by the court or represented by a public defender hired by the state.

Aside from the civil and criminal cases, there are other matters which require bringing to court and these relate to petitions in special proceedings or administrative matters which may be taken up with quasi-judicial or administrative bodies. But the purpose of your seeking reliefs or remedies under either of the fora is the same—the quest for justice.

Hierarchy of courts

There are several steps in the judicial ladder. In the Philippines, cases commence either at the first or second level courts. Then they may be elevated to the collegiate courts and ultimately to the highest court of the land. The municipal trial courts constitute the first level courts while the regional trial courts make up the second level courts. Appellate level courts in the Philippines are the Court of Appeals, *Sandiganbayan* (anti-graft court) and the Court of Tax Appeals. The highest court in the country is the Supreme Court of the Philippines. In certain cases, however, the regional trial courts serve as appellate courts to the municipal trial courts.

Instituting an action in court

To validly file a case in court, you must have a cause of action. Philippine jurisprudence defines cause of action as "an act or omission of one party in violation of the legal right or rights of another." The elements of a cause of action are: (1) a right in favor of the plaintiff by whatever means and under whatever law it arises or is created; (2) an obligation on the part of the named defendant to respect or not to violate such right; and (3) an act or omission on the part of such defendant in violation of the right of the plaintiff or constituting a breach of the obligations of the defendant to the plaintiff for which the latter may maintain an action for recovery of damages. (*GR 140825, 13 Oct 00*)

Action means *an ordinary suit in a court of justice,* by which one party prosecutes another for the enforcement or protection of a right, or the prevention or redress of a wrong. "xxx An action is a formal demand of one's legal rights in a court of justice in the manner prescribed by the court or by the law. xxx" It is clear that the determinative or operative fact which converts a claim into an "action or suit" is the filing of the same with a "court of justice." Filed elsewhere, as with some other body or office not a court of justice, the claim may not be categorized under either term. Unlike an action, an extrajudicial foreclosure of real estate mortgage is initiated by filing a petition not with any court of justice but with the office of the sheriff of the province where the sale is to be made. By no stretch of the imagination can the office of the sheriff come under the category of a court of justice. And as aptly observed by the complainant, if ever the executive judge comes into the picture, it is only because he exercises administrative supervision over the sheriff. But this administrative supervision, however, does not change the fact that extrajudicial foreclosures are not judicial proceedings, actions or suits. (*AM RTJ-93-1031, 28 Jan 97*)

In determining whether allegations of a complaint are sufficient to support a cause of action, it must be borne in mind that the complaint does not have to establish or allege facts proving the existence of a cause of action at the outset; this will have to be done at the trial on the merits of the case. To sustain a motion to dismiss for lack of cause of action, the complaint must show that the claim for relief does not exist, rather than that a claim has been defectively stated, or is ambiguous, indefinite or uncertain. (*GR111538, 26 Feb 97*)

It is a well-settled rule that the existence of a cause of action is determined by the allegations in the complaint. In the resolution of a motion to dismiss based on failure to state a cause of action, only the facts alleged in the complaint must be considered. The test in cases like these is whether a court can render a valid judgment on the complaint based upon the facts alleged and pursuant to the prayer therein. Hence, it has been held that a motion to dismiss generally partakes of the nature of a demurrer which hypothetically admits the truth of the factual allegations made in a complaint. (*GR 117029, 19 Mar 97*)

It is axiomatic nonetheless that a court has a mandate to apply relevant statutes and jurisprudence in determining whether the allegations in a complaint establish a cause of action. While it focuses on the complaint, a court clearly cannot disregard decisions material to the proper appreciation of the questions before it. (*Ibid.*)

Jurisdiction

It is important to be apprised which court has jurisdiction over your case. Thus, it pays to know how the subject matter of jurisdiction is tackled in jurisprudence.

Jurisdiction is the authority to hear and determine a cause—the right to act in a case. As distinguished from the exercise of jurisdiction, jurisdiction is the authority to decide a cause, and not the decision rendered therein. Where there is jurisdiction over the person and the subject matter, the decision on all other questions arising in the case is but an exercise of that jurisdiction. And the errors which a court or officer may commit in the exercise of such jurisdiction are merely errors of judgment. The traditional distinction is that error of jurisdiction may be reviewed in *certiorari* proceedings; while errors of judgment can be corrected only by appeal. (*GR 131047, 2 Mar 99*)

Jurisdiction is more substantive than procedural. It refers to the authority of the court to hear and decide a case, and, it is one that is dictated by law, and the matter ordinarily can be raised at any stage of the trial, even upon appeal. The rule, of course, deviates from this general rule in criminal cases where *locus criminis* itself defines the jurisdiction of the trial court. (*GR 142523, 27 Nov 01*)

It is axiomatic that what determines the nature of an action as well as which court has jurisdiction over it, are the allegations in the complaint and the character of the relief sought. "Jurisdiction over the subject matter is determined upon the allegations made in the complaint, irrespective of whether the plaintiff is entitled to recover upon a claim asserted therein - a matter resolved only after and as a result of the trial. Neither can the jurisdiction of the court be made to depend upon the defenses made by the defendant in his answer or motion to dismiss. If such were the rule, the question of jurisdiction would depend almost entirely upon the defendant." (*GR 123417, 10 Jun 99*)

Jurisdiction over the subject matter or nature of an action is conferred only by law. It may not be conferred by consent or waiver upon a court which otherwise would have no jurisdiction over the subject matter of an action. On the other hand, the venue of an action as fixed by statute may be changed by the consent of the parties, and an objection on improper venue may be waived by the failure of the defendant to raise it at the proper time. In such an event, the court may still render a valid judgment. Rules as to jurisdiction can never be left to the consent or agreement of the parties. Venue is procedural, not jurisdictional, and hence may be waived. It is meant to provide convenience to the parties, rather than restrict their access to the courts as it relates to the place of trial. (*GR 133240, 15 Nov 00*)

Aspects of litigation

Strict adherence to procedural rules must at all times be observed. However, it is not the end-all and be-all of litigation. (*GR 47013, 17 Feb 00*)

While it is true that a litigation is not a game of technicalities, it is equally true that every case must be prosecuted in accordance with the prescribed procedure to ensure an orderly and speedy administration of justice. There have been some instances wherein the Supreme Court allowed a relaxation in the application of the rules, but this flexibility was "never intended to forge a bastion for erring litigants to violate the rules with impunity." A liberal interpretation and application of the rules of procedure can be resorted to only in proper cases and under justifiable causes and circumstances. (*GR 131457, 17 Nov 98*)

Venue

Venue refers to the place where your action is instituted.

As practiced in the Philippines, the complaint in personal actions may be filed in the place where the defendant resides or may be found, or where plaintiff resides, at the option of the plaintiff. The Rules give the plaintiff the option of choosing where to file his complaint. He can file it in the place (1) where he himself or any of them resides; or (2) where the defendant or any of the defendants resides or may be found. The plaintiff or the defendant must be residents of the place where the action has been instituted at the time the action is commenced. (*GR 100748, 3 Feb 97*)

The residence of a person must be his personal, actual or physical habitation or his actual residence or abode. It does not mean fixed permanent residence to which when absent, one has the intention of returning. The word "resides" connotes ex vi termini "actual residence" as distinguished from "legal residence" or "domicile." Actual residence may in some cases be the legal residence or domicile, but for purposes of venue, actual residence is the place of abode and not necessarily legal residence or domicile. Actual residence signifies personal residence, *i.e.*, physical presence and actual stay thereat. This physical presence, nonetheless, must be more than temporary and must be with continuity and consistency. (*Ibid.*)

Real actions, as so opposed to personal actions, are those which affect the title to or possession of real property. Where a contrary claim to ownership is made by an adverse party, and where the relief prayed for cannot be granted without the court deciding on the merits the issue of ownership and title, more specifically so as to who, between the contending parties, would have a better right to the property, the case can only be but a real action. (*GR 142523, supra*)

It is fundamental that the situs for bringing real and personal civil actions is fixed by the rules to attain the greatest convenience possible to parties litigants and their witnesses by affording them maximum accessibility to the courts of justice. The choice of venue is given to the plaintiff but is not left to his caprice. It cannot unduly deprive a resident defendant of the rights conferred upon him by the Rules of Court. (*GR 100748, supra*)

Parties

A real party in interest is defined as "the party who stands to be benefited or injured by the judgment or the party entitled to the avails of the suit."

"Interest" within the meaning of the rule means material interest, an interest in issue and to be affected by the decree, as distinguished from mere interest in the question involved, or a mere incidental interest. By real interest is meant a present substantial interest, as distinguished from a mere expectancy or a future, contingent, subordinate, or consequential interest. (*GR 126102, 4 Dec 00*)

Legal standing means a personal and substantial interest in the case such that the party has sustained or will sustain direct injury as a result of x x x the act being challenged. The term 'interest' is material interest, an interest in issue and to be affected by the decree, as distinguished from mere interest in the question involved, or a mere incidental interest. Moreover, the interest of the party must be personal and not one based on a desire to vindicate the constitutional right of some third and unrelated party." (*GR 131277, 2 Feb 99*)

An indispensable party is one whose interest will be affected by the court's action in the litigation, and without whom no final determination of the case can be had. The party's interest in the subject matter of the suit and in the relief sought are so inextricably intertwined with the other parties that his legal presence as a party to the proceeding is an absolute necessity. In his absence, there cannot be a resolution of the dispute of the parties before the Court which is effective, complete, or equitable. (*GR 110048, 19 Nov 99*)

Conversely, a party is not indispensable to the suit if his interest in the controversy or subject matter is distinct and divisible from the interest of the other parties and will not necessarily be prejudiced by a judgment which does complete justice to the parties in Court. He is not indispensable if his presence would merely complete relief between him and those already parties to the action or will simply avoid multiple litigation. Without the presence of indispensable parties to a suit or proceeding, a judgment of a Court cannot attain real finality. (*Ibid.*)

Administrative remedies, need to avail

Courts, for reasons of law, comity and convenience, should not entertain suits unless the available administrative remedies have first been resorted to and the proper authorities have been given an appropriate opportunity to act and correct their alleged errors, if any, committed in the administrative forum. (*GR 93540, 13 Dec 99*)

The thrust of the rule on exhaustion of administrative remedies is that the courts must allow the administrative agencies to carry out their functions and discharge their responsibilities within the specialized areas of their respective competence. It is presumed that an administrative agency, if afforded an opportunity to pass upon a matter, will decide the same correctly, or correct any previous error committed in its forum. Furthermore, reasons of law, comity and convenience prevent the courts from entertaining cases proper for determination by administrative agencies. Hence, premature resort to the courts necessarily becomes fatal to the cause of action of the petitioner. (*GR 106028, 9 May 01*)

The doctrine of exhaustion of administrative remedies is not without its practical and legal reasons. Indeed, resort to administrative remedies entails lesser expenses and provides for speedier disposition of controversies. Our courts of justice for reason of comity and convenience will shy away from a dispute until the system of administrative redress has been completed and complied with so as to give the administrative agency every opportunity to correct its error and to dispose of the case. (*GR 109853, 11 Oct 00*)

True, the principle of exhaustion of administrative remedies has certain exceptions as embodied in various cases. This doctrine is a relative one and is flexible depending on the peculiarity and uniqueness of the factual and circumstantial settings of a case. It is disregarded: (1) when there is a violation of due process; (2) when the issue involved is purely a legal question; (3) when the administrative action is patently illegal and amounts to lack or excess of jurisdiction; (4) when there is estoppel on the part of the administrative agency concerned; (5) when there is irreparable injury; (6) when the respondent is a department secretary whose acts, as an alter ego of the President, bears the implied and assumed approval of the latter; (7) when to require exhaustion of administrative remedies would be unreasonable; (8) when it would amount to a nullification of a claim; (9) when the subject matter is a private land in land case proceedings; (10) when the rule does not provide a plain, speedy and adequate remedy; (11) when there are circumstances indicating the urgency of judicial intervention; and unreasonable delay would greatly prejudice the complainant; (12) when no administrative review is provided by law; (13) where the rule of qualified political agency applies; and (14) when the issue of non-exhaustion of administrative remedies has been rendered moot. (*Ibid.*)

The underlying principle of the rule of exhaustion of administrative remedies rests on the presumption that the administrative agency, if afforded a complete chance to pass upon the matter, will decide the same correctly. There are both legal and practical reasons for the principle. The administrative process is intended to provide less expensive and more speedy solutions to disputes. Where the enabling statute indicates a procedure for administrative review and provides a system of administrative appeal or reconsideration, the court--for reason of law, comity, and convenience--will not entertain a case unless the available administrative remedies have been resorted to and the appropriate authorities have been given an opportunity to act and correct the errors committed in the administrative forum. (*GR 131729, 19 May 98*)

Chapter 2
Courts and Lawyers

The court's jurisdiction is conferred either by the Constitution or by Congress. Thus—

Outside the cases enumerated in xxx the Constitution, Congress has the plenary power to define, prescribe and apportion the jurisdiction of various courts. Accordingly, Congress may, by law, provide that a certain class of cases should be exclusively heard and determined by one court. Such would be a special law and must be construed as an exception to the general law on jurisdiction of courts. (*GR 126623, 12 Dec 97*)

Judicial power "includes the duty of the courts of justice to settle actual controversies involving rights which are legally demandable and enforceable." Such is provided in the Philippine Constitution. Judicial review, which is merely an aspect of judicial power, demands the following: (1) there must be an actual case calling for the exercise of judicial power; (2) the question must be ripe for adjudication; and (3) the person challenging must have "standing"; that is, he has personal and substantial interest in the case, such that he has sustained or will sustain direct injury. (GR 125532, 10 Jul 98)

The first requisite is that there must be before a court an actual case calling for the exercise of judicial power. Courts have no authority to pass upon issues through advisory opinions or to resolve hypothetical or feigned problems or friendly suits collusively arranged between parties without real adverse interests. Courts do not sit to adjudicate mere academic questions to satisfy scholarly interest, however intellectually challenging. As a condition precedent to the exercise of judicial power, an actual controversy between litigants must first exist. (*Ibid.*)

An actual case or controversy exists when there is a conflict of legal rights or an assertion of opposite legal claims, which can be resolved on the basis of existing law and jurisprudence. A justiciable controversy is distinguished from a hypothetical or abstract difference or dispute, in that the former involves a definite and concrete dispute touching on the legal relations of parties having adverse legal interests. A justiciable controversy admits of specific relief through a decree that is conclusive in character, whereas an opinion only advises what the law would be upon a hypothetical state of facts.(*Ibid.*)

Factual findings of the trial court, when adopted and confirmed by the Court of Appeals, are final and conclusive and may not be reviewed on appeal; except: (1) when the inference made is manifestly mistaken, absurd or impossible; (2) when there is a grave abuse of discretion; (3) when the finding is grounded entirely on speculations, surmises or conjectures; (4) when the judgment of the Court of Appeals is based on misapprehension of facts; (5) when the findings of fact are conflicting; (6) when the Court of Appeals, in making its findings, went beyond the issues of the case and the same is contrary to the admissions of both appellant and appellee; (7) when the findings of the Court of Appeals are contrary to those of the trial court; (8) when the findings of fact are conclusions without citation of specific evidence on which they are based; (9) when the Court of Appeals manifestly overlooked certain relevant facts not disputed by the parties and which, if properly considered, would justify a different conclusion; and (10) when the findings of fact of the Court of Appeals are premised on the absence of evidence and are contradicted by the evidence on record. (*GR 112550, 5 Feb 01*)

Lawyer-client relationship

The practice of law is so intimately affected with public interest that it is both a right and a duty of the State to control and regulate it in order to promote the public welfare. The Constitution vests this power of control and regulation in the Supreme Court. Since the practice of law is inseparably connected with the exercise of its judicial power in administration of justice, the Court cannot be divested of its constitutionally ordained prerogative which includes the authority to discipline, suspend or disbar any unfit and unworthy member of the Bar by a mere execution of affidavits of voluntary desistance and quitclaim.

A lawyer shall at all times uphold the integrity and dignity of the legal profession. The bar should maintain a high standard of legal proficiency as well as of honesty and fair dealing. A lawyer brings honor to the legal profession by faithfully performing his duties to society, to the bar, to the courts and to his clients. To this end a member of the legal fraternity should refrain from doing any act which might lessen in any degree the confidence and trust reposed by the public in the fidelity, honesty and integrity of the legal profession. (*AC 4539, 14 May 97*)

While a lawyer owes absolute fidelity to the cause of his client, full devotion to his genuine interest, and warm zeal in the maintenance and defense of his rights, as well as the exertion of his utmost learning and ability, he must do so only within the bounds of the law. He must give a candid and honest opinion on the merits and probable results of his client's case with the end in view of promoting respect for the law and legal processes, and counsel or maintain such actions or proceedings only as appear to him to be just, and such defenses only as he believes to be honestly debatable under the law. He must always remind himself of the oath he took upon admission to the Bar that he "will not wittingly or willingly promote or sue any groundless, false or unlawful suit nor give aid nor consent to the same"; and that he "will conduct [himself] as a lawyer according to the best of [his] knowledge and discretion with all good fidelity as well to the courts as to [his] clients." Needless to state, the lawyer's fidelity to his client must not be pursued at the expense of truth and the administration of justice, and it must be done within the bounds of reason and common sense. A lawyer's responsibility to protect and advance the interests of his client does not warrant a course of action propelled by ill motives and malicious intentions against the other party. (*AM MTJ-95-1063, 9 Aug 96*)

In modern day perception of the lawyer-client relationship, an attorney is more than a mere agent or servant, because he possesses special powers of trust and confidence reposed on him by his client. A lawyer is also as independent as the judge of the court, thus his powers are entirely different from and superior to those of an ordinary agent. Moreover, an attorney also occupies what may be considered as a "quasi-judicial office" since he is in fact an officer of the Court and exercises his judgment in the choice of courses of action to be taken favorable to his client. Thus, in the creation of lawyer-client relationship, there are rules, ethical conduct and duties that breathe life into it, among those, the fiduciary duty to his client which is of a very delicate, exacting and confidential character, requiring a very high degree of fidelity and good faith, that is required by reason of necessity and public interest based on the hypothesis that abstinence from seeking legal advice in a good cause is an evil which is fatal to the administration of justice. (*GR 105938 & 108113, 20 Sep 96*)

It is also the strict sense of fidelity of a lawyer to his client that distinguishes him from any other professional in society. This conception is entrenched and embodies centuries of established and stable tradition. (*Ibid.*)

In **Stockton v. Ford**, *52 U.S. (11 How.) 232, 247, 13 L. Ed. 676 (1850)*, the U.S. Supreme Court held:

There are few of the business relations of life involving a higher trust and confidence than that of attorney and client, or generally speaking, one more honorably and faithfully discharged; few more anxiously guarded by the law, or governed by the sterner principles of morality and justice; and it is the duty of the court to administer them in a corresponding spirit, and to be watchful and industrious, to see that confidence thus reposed shall not be used to the detriment or prejudice of the rights of the party bestowing it. (*Ibid.*)

In *GR 105938 & 108113*, the ruling of the Supreme Court of the Philippines likewise states:

Considerations favoring confidentiality in lawyer-client relationships are many and serve several constitutional and policy concerns. In the constitutional sphere, the privilege gives flesh to one of the most sacrosanct rights available to the accused, the right to counsel. If a client were made to choose between legal representation without effective communication and disclosure and legal representation with all his secrets revealed then he might be compelled, in some instances, to either opt to stay away from the judicial system or to lose the right to counsel. If the price of disclosure is too high, or if it amounts to self incrimination, then the flow of information would be curtailed thereby rendering the right practically nugatory. The threat this represents against another sacrosanct individual right, the right to be presumed innocent is at once self-evident.

Encouraging full disclosure to a lawyer by one seeking legal services opens the door to a whole spectrum of legal options which would otherwise be circumscribed by limited information engendered by a fear of disclosure. An effective lawyer-client relationship is largely dependent upon the degree of confidence which exists between lawyer and client which in turn requires a situation which encourages a dynamic and fruitful exchange and flow of information. It necessarily follows that in order to attain effective representation, the lawyer must invoke the privilege not as a matter of option but as a matter of duty and professional responsibility.

As a matter of public policy, a client's identity should not be shrouded in mystery. Under this premise, the general rule in our jurisdiction as well as in the United States is that a lawyer may not invoke the privilege and refuse to divulge the name or identity of his client.

The reasons advanced for the general rule are well established.

First, the court has a right to know that the client whose privileged information is sought to be protected is flesh and blood.

Second, the privilege begins to exist only after the attorney-client relationship has been established. The attorney-client privilege does not attach until there is a client.

Third, the privilege generally pertains to the *subject matter* of the relationship.

Finally, due process considerations require that the opposing party should, as a general rule, know his adversary. "A party suing or sued is entitled to know who his opponent is." He cannot be obliged to grope in the dark against unknown forces.

Notwithstanding these considerations, the general rule is however qualified by some important exceptions.

1) Client identity is privileged where a strong probability exists that revealing the client's name would implicate that client in the very activity for which he sought the lawyer's advice.

In *Ex-Parte Enzor,* a state supreme court reversed a lower court order requiring a lawyer to divulge the name of her client on the ground that the subject matter of the relationship was so closely related to the issue of the client's identity that the privilege actually attached to both. In *Enzor*, the unidentified client, an election official, informed his attorney in confidence that he had been offered a bribe to violate election laws or that he had accepted a bribe to that end. In her testimony, the attorney revealed that she had advised her client to count the votes correctly, but averred that she could not remember whether her client had been, in fact, bribed. The lawyer was cited for contempt for her refusal to reveal his client's identity before a grand jury. Reversing the lower court's contempt orders, the state supreme court held that under the circumstances of the case, and under the exceptions described above, even the name of the client was privileged.

U.S. v. Hodge and Zweig, involved the same exception, i.e. that client identity is privileged in those instances where a strong probability exists that the disclosure of the client's identity would implicate the client in the very criminal activity for which the lawyer's legal advice was obtained.

The *Hodge* case involved federal grand jury proceedings inquiring into the activities of the "Sandino Gang," a gang involved in the illegal importation of drugs in the United States. The respondents, law partners, represented key witnesses and suspects including the leader of the gang, Joe Sandino.

In connection with a tax investigation in November of 1973, the IRS issued summons to Hodge and Zweig, requiring them to produce documents and information regarding payment received by Sandino on behalf of any other person, and vice versa. The lawyers refused to divulge the names. The Ninth Circuit of the United States Court of Appeals, upholding non-disclosure under the facts and circumstances of the case, held:

A client's identity and the nature of that client's fee arrangements may be privileged where the person invoking the privilege can show that a strong probability exists that disclosure of such information would implicate that client in the very criminal activity for which legal advice was sought *Baird v. Koerner*, 279 F.2d at 680. While in Baird Owe enunciated this rule as a matter of California law, the rule also reflects federal law. Appellants contend that the *Baird* exception applies to this case.

The *Baird* exception is entirely consonant with the principal policy behind the attorney-client privilege. "In order to promote freedom of consultation of legal advisors by clients, the apprehension of compelled disclosure from the legal advisors must be removed; hence, the law must prohibit such disclosure except on the client's consent." 8 J. *Wigmore, supra, sec. 2291, at 545.* In furtherance of this policy, the client's identity and the nature of his fee arrangements are, in exceptional cases, protected as confidential communications.

2) Where disclosure would open the client to civil liability, his identity is privileged. For instance, the peculiar facts and circumstances of *Neugass v. Terminal Cab Corporation,* prompted the New York Supreme Court to allow a lawyer's claim to the effect that he could not reveal the name of his client because this would expose the latter to civil litigation.

In the said case, Neugass, the plaintiff, suffered injury when the taxicab she was riding, owned by respondent corporation, collided with a second taxicab, whose owner was unknown. Plaintiff brought action against both defendant corporation and the owner of the second cab, identified in the information only as John Doe. It turned out that when the attorney of defendant corporation appeared on preliminary examination, the fact was somehow revealed that the lawyer came to know the name of the owner of the second cab when a man, a client of the insurance company, prior to the institution of legal action, came to him and reported that he was involved in a car accident. It was apparent under the circumstances that the man was the owner of the second cab. The state supreme court held that the reports were clearly made to the lawyer in his professional capacity. The court said:

That his employment came about through the fact that the insurance company had hired him to defend its policyholders seems immaterial. The attorney in such cases is clearly the attorney for the policyholder when the policyholder goes to him to report an occurrence contemplating that it would be used in an action or claim against him. x x x

All communications made by a client to his counsel, for the purpose of professional advice or assistance, are privileged, whether they relate to a suit pending or contemplated, or to any other matter proper for such advice or aid; x x x And whenever the communication made, relates to a matter so connected with the employment as attorney or counsel as to afford presumption that it was the ground of the address by the client, then it is privileged from disclosure. xxx.

It appears... that the name and address of the owner of the second cab came to the attorney in this case as a confidential communication. His client is not seeking to use the courts, and his address cannot be disclosed on that theory, nor is the present action pending against him as service of the summons on him has not been effected. The objections on which the court reserved decision are sustained.

In the case of *Matter of Shawmut Mining Company,* the lawyer involved was required by a lower court to disclose whether he represented certain clients in a certain transaction. The purpose of the court's request was to determine whether the unnamed persons as interested parties were

30

connected with the purchase of properties involved in the action. The lawyer refused and brought the question to the State Supreme Court. Upholding the lawyer's refusal to divulge the names of his clients the court held:

If it can compel the witness to state, as directed by the order appealed from, that he represented certain persons in the purchase or sale of these mines, it has made progress in establishing by such evidence their version of the litigation. As already suggested, such testimony by the witness would compel him to disclose not only that he was attorney for certain people, but that, as the result of communications made to him in the course of such employment as such attorney, he knew that they were interested in certain transactions. We feel sure that under such conditions no case has ever gone to the length of compelling an attorney, at the instance of a hostile litigant, to disclose not only his retainer, but the nature of the transactions to which it related, when such information could be made the basis of a suit against his client.

3) Where the government's lawyers have no case against an attorney's client unless, by revealing the client's name, the said name would furnish the only link that would form the chain of testimony necessary to convict an individual of a crime, the client's name is privileged.

In *Baird vs Korner,* a lawyer was consulted by the accountants and the lawyer of certain undisclosed taxpayers regarding steps to be taken to place the undisclosed taxpayers in a favorable position in case criminal charges were brought against them by the U.S. Internal Revenue Service (IRS).

It appeared that the taxpayers' returns of previous years were probably incorrect and the taxes understated. The clients themselves were unsure about whether or not they violated tax laws and sought advice from Baird on the hypothetical possibility that they had. No investigation was then being undertaken by the IRS of the taxpayers. Subsequently, the attorney of the taxpayers delivered to Baird the sum of $12,706.85, which had been previously assessed as the tax due, and another amount of money representing his fee for the advice given. Baird then sent a check for $12,706.85 to the IRS in Baltimore, Maryland, with a note explaining the payment, but without naming his clients. The IRS demanded that Baird identify the lawyers, accountants, and other clients involved. Baird refused on the ground that he did not know their names, and declined to name the attorney and accountants because this constituted privileged communication. A petition was filed for the enforcement of the IRS summons. For Baird's repeated refusal to name his clients he was found guilty of civil contempt. The Ninth Circuit Court of Appeals held that, a lawyer could not be forced to reveal the names of clients who employed him to pay sums of money to the government voluntarily in settlement of undetermined income taxes, unsued on, and with no government audit or investigation into that client's income tax liability pending. The court emphasized the exception that a client's name is privileged when so much has been revealed concerning the legal services rendered that the disclosure of the client's identity exposes him to possible investigation and sanction by government agencies. The Court held:

The facts of the instant case bring it squarely within that exception to the general rule. Here money was received by the government, paid by persons who thereby admitted they had not paid a sufficient amount in income taxes some one or more years in the past. The names of the clients are useful to the government for but one purpose - to ascertain which taxpayers think they were delinquent, so that it may check the records for that one year or several years. The voluntary nature of the payment indicates a belief by the taxpayers that more taxes or interest or penalties are due than the sum previously paid, if any. It indicates a feeling of guilt for nonpayment of taxes, though whether it is criminal guilt is undisclosed. But it may well be the link that could form the chain of testimony necessary to convict an individual of a federal crime. Certainly the payment and the feeling of guilt are the reasons the attorney here involved was employed - to advise his clients what, under the circumstances, should be done.

Apart from these principal exceptions, there exist other situations which could qualify as exceptions to the general rule. For example, the content of any client communication to a lawyer lies within the privilege if it is relevant to the subject matter of the legal problem on which the client seeks legal assistance. Moreover, where the *nature* of the attorney-client relationship has been previously disclosed *and it is the identity which is intended to be confidential*, the identity of the client has been held to be privileged, since such revelation would otherwise result in disclosure of the entire transaction.

Summarizing these exceptions, information relating to the identity of a client may fall within the ambit of the privilege when the client's name itself has an independent significance, such that disclosure would then reveal client confidences.

The circumstances involving the engagement of lawyers in the case at bench, therefore, clearly reveal that the instant case falls under at least two exceptions to the general rule. First, disclosure of the alleged client's name would lead to establish said client's connection with the very fact in issue of the case, which is privileged information, because the privilege, as stated earlier, protects the subject matter or the substance (without which there would be no attorney-client relationship).

The link between the alleged criminal offense and the legal advice or legal service sought was duly established in the case at bar, by no less than the PCGG itself. The key lies in the three specific conditions laid down by the PCGG which constitutes petitioners' ticket to non-prosecution should they accede thereto: (a) the disclosure of the identity of its clients; (b) submission of documents substantiating the lawyer-client relationship; and (c) the submission of the deeds of assignment petitioners executed in favor of their clients covering their respective shareholdings.

From these conditions, particularly the third, we can readily deduce that the clients indeed consulted the petitioners, in their capacity as lawyers, regarding the financial and corporate structure, framework and set-up of the corporations in question. In turn, petitioners gave their professional advice in the form of, among others, the aforementioned deeds of assignment covering their clients' shareholdings.

There is no question that the preparation of the aforestated documents was part and parcel of petitioners' legal service to their clients. More important, it constituted an integral part of their duties as lawyers. Petitioners, therefore, have a legitimate fear that identifying their clients would implicate them in the very activity for which legal advice had been sought, i.e., the alleged accumulation of ill-gotten wealth in the aforementioned corporations.

Furthermore, under the third main exception, revelation of the client's name would obviously provide the necessary link for the prosecution to build its case, where none otherwise exists. It is the link, in the words of *Baird,* "that would inevitably form the chain of testimony necessary to convict the (client) of a... crime."

An important distinction must be made between a case where a client takes on the services of an attorney for illicit purposes, seeking advice about how to go around the law for the purpose of committing illegal activities and a case where a client thinks he might have previously committed something illegal and consults his attorney about it. The first case clearly does not fall within the privilege because the same cannot be invoked for purposes illegal. The second case falls within the exception because whether or not the act for which the advice turns out to be illegal, his name cannot be used or disclosed if the disclosure leads to evidence, not yet in the hands of the prosecution, which might lead to possible action against him.

These cases may be readily distinguished, because the privilege cannot be invoked or used as a shield for an illegal act, as in the first example; while the prosecution may not have a case against the client in the second example and cannot use the attorney client relationship to build up a case against the latter. The reason for the first rule is that it is not within the professional character of a lawyer to give advice on the commission of a crime. The reason for the second has been stated in the cases above discussed and are founded on the same policy grounds for which the attorney-client privilege, in general, exists.

In *Matter of Shawmut Mining Co., supra,* the appellate court therein stated that "under such conditions no case has ever yet gone to the length of compelling an attorney, at the instance of a hostile litigant, to disclose not only his retainer, but the nature of the transactions to which it related, when such information could be made the basis of a suit against his client."

"Communications made to an attorney **in the course of any personal employment, relating to the subject thereof**, and which may be supposed to be drawn out in consequence of the relation in which the parties stand to each other, are under the seal of confidence and entitled to protection as privileged communications." Where the communicated information, which clearly falls within the privilege, would suggest possible criminal activity but there would be not much in the information known to the prosecution which would sustain a charge except that revealing the name of the client would open up other privileged information which would substantiate the prosecution's suspicions, then the client's identity is so inextricably linked to the subject matter itself that it falls within the protection. The *Baird* exception, applicable to the instant case, is consonant with the principal policy behind the privilege, i.e., that for the purpose of promoting freedom of consultation of legal advisors by clients, apprehension of compelled disclosure from attorneys must be eliminated. This exception has likewise been sustained in *In re Grand Jury Proceedings* and *Tillotson v. Boughner.*

What these cases unanimously seek to avoid is the exploitation of the general rule in what may amount to a fishing expedition by the prosecution.

There are, after all, alternative sources of information available to the prosecutor which do not depend on utilizing a defendant's counsel as a convenient and readily available source of information in the building of a case against the latter. Compelling disclosure of the client's name in circumstances such as the one which exists in the case at bench amounts to sanctioning fishing expeditions by lazy prosecutors and litigants which we cannot and will not countenance. When the nature of the transaction would be revealed by disclosure of an attorney's retainer, such retainer is obviously protected by the privilege. It follows that petitioner attorneys in the instant case owe their client(s) a duty and an obligation not to disclose the latter's identity which in turn requires them to invoke the privilege.

In fine, the crux of petitioners' objections ultimately hinges on their expectation that if the prosecution has a case against their clients, the latter's case should be built upon evidence painstakingly gathered by them from their own sources and not from compelled testimony requiring them to reveal the name of their clients, information which unavoidably reveals much about the nature of the transaction which may or may not be illegal. The logical nexus between name and nature of transaction is so intimate in this case that it would be difficult to simply dissociate one from the other. In this sense, the name is as much "communication" as information revealed directly about the transaction in question itself, a communication which is clearly and distinctly privileged. A lawyer cannot reveal such communication without exposing himself to charges of violating a principle which forms the bulwark of the entire attorney-client relationship.

The *uberrimei fidei* relationship between a lawyer and his client therefore imposes a strict liability for negligence on the former. The ethical duties owing to the client, including confidentiality, loyalty, competence, diligence as well asthe responsibility to keep clients informed and protect their rights to make decisions have been zealously sustained. In *Milbank, Tweed, Hadley and McCloy v. Boon*, the US Second District Court rejected the plea of the petitioner law firm that it breached its fiduciary duty to its client by helping the latter's former agent in closing a deal for the agent's benefit only after its client hesitated in proceeding with the transaction, thus causing no harm to its client. The Court instead ruled that breaches of a fiduciary relationship in any context comprise a special breed of cases that often loosen normally stringent requirements of causation and damages, and found in favor of the client.

To the same effect is the ruling in *Searcy, Denney, Scarola, Barnhart, and Shipley P.A. v. Scheller* requiring strict obligation of lawyers *vis-a-vis* clients. In this case, a contingent fee lawyer was fired shortly before the end of completion of his work, and sought payment *quantum meruit* of work done. The court, however, found that the lawyer was fired for cause after he sought to pressure his client into signing a new fee agreement while settlement negotiations were at a critical stage.

While the client found a new lawyer during the *interregnum*, events forced the client to settle for less than what was originally offered. Reiterating the principle of fiduciary duty of lawyers to clients in *Meinhard v. Salmon* famously attributed to Justice Benjamin Cardozo that "Not honesty alone, but the *punctilio* of an honor the most sensitive, is then the standard of behavior," the US Court found that the lawyer involved was fired for cause, thus deserved no attorney's fees at all.

The utmost zeal given by Courts to the protection of the lawyer-client confidentiality privilege and lawyer's loyalty to his client is evident in the duration of the protection, which exists not only during the relationship, but extends even after the termination of the relationship.

Such are the unrelenting duties required of lawyers *vis-a-vis* their clients because the law, which the lawyers are sworn to uphold, in the words of Oliver Wendell Holmes, "xxx is an exacting goddess, demanding of her votaries in intellectual and moral discipline." The Court, no less, is not prepared to accept respondents' position without denigrating the noble profession that is lawyering, so extolled by Justice Holmes in this wise:

Every calling is great when greatly pursued. But what other gives such scope to realize the spontaneous energy of one's soul? In what other does one plunge so deep in the stream of life - so share its passions its battles, its despair, its triumphs, both as witness and actor? x x x But that is not all. What a subject is this in which we are united - this abstraction called the Law, wherein as in a magic mirror, we see reflected, not only in our lives, but the lives of all men that have been. When I think on this majestic theme my eyes dazzle. If we are to speak of the law as our mistress, we who are here know that she is a mistress only to be won with sustained and lonely passion - only to be won by straining all the faculties by which man is likened to God.

We have no choice but to uphold petitioners' right not to reveal the identity of their clients under pain of the breach of fiduciary duty owing to their clients, because the facts of the instant case clearly fall within recognized exceptions to the rule that the client's name is not privileged information. (*Citations Omitted*)

Notarization

Notarization is not an empty, meaningless, routinary act. It is invested with substantive public interest, such that only those who are qualified or authorized may act as notaries public. The protection of that interest necessarily requires that those not qualified or authorized to act must be prevented from imposing upon the public, the courts, and the administrative offices in general. It must be underscored that the notarization by a notary public converts a private document into a public document making that document admissible in evidence without further proof of the authenticity thereof. A notarial document is by law entitled to full faith and credit upon its face. (*AC 4758, 30 Apr 99*)

The function of a notary public is, among others, to guard against any illegal or immoral arrangements. (*AM P-99-1338, 18 Nov 99*)

The acknowledgment shall be made before a notary public or an officer duly authorized by law of the country to take acknowledgments of instruments or documents in the place where the act is done. The notary public or the officer taking the acknowledgment shall certify that the person acknowledging the instrument or document is known to him and that he is the same person who executed it, and acknowledged that the same is his free act and deed. The certificate shall be made under the official seal, if he is by law required to keep a seal, and if not, his certificate shall so state. (*AC 4539, 14 May 97*)

Chapter 3
Court Appearances, Pleadings, and Motions

Pleadings

Pleadings are the written statements of the respective claims and defenses of the parties submitted to the court for appropriate judgment. The claims of a party are asserted in a complaint, counterclaim, cross-claim, third (fourth, etc.)—party complaint, or complaint-in-intervention. The defenses of a party are alleged in the answer to the pleading asserting a claim against him. An answer may be responded to by a reply. The complaint is the pleading alleging the plaintiff's cause or causes of action. An answer is a pleading in which a defending party sets fourth his defenses. (*As defined in Rules of Court for Philippine Courts, Sec.6*)

A counterclaim is any claim which a defending party may have against an opposing party. A cross-claim is any claim by one party against a co-party arising out of the transaction or occurrence that is the subject matter either of the original action or of a counterclaim therein. Such cross-claim may include a claim that the party against whom it is asserted is or may be liable to the cross-claimant for all or part of a claim asserted in the action against the cross-claimant. (*Ibid.*)

A reply is a pleading, the office or function of which is to deny, or allege facts in denial or avoidance of new matters alleged by way of defense in the answer and thereby join or make issue as to such new matters. If a party does not file such reply, all the new matters alleged in the answer are deemed controverted. If the plaintiff whishes to interpose any claims arising out of the new matters so alleged such claims shall be set forth in an amended or supplemental complaint. (*Ibid.*)

Motions

When one applies for a relief other than by a pleading before the court, such application is known as a motion. A defendant, within the time for but before filing the answer to the complaint or pleading asserting a claim, may interpose a motion to dismiss on any of the following grounds: (a) That the court has no jurisdiction over the person of the defending party;(b) That the court has no jurisdiction over the subject matter of the claim; (c) That venue is improperly laid; (d) That the plaintiff has no legal capacity to sue; (e) That there is another action pending between the same parties for the same cause; (f) That the cause of action is barred by a prior judgment or by the statute of limitations; (g) That the pleading asserting the claim states no cause of action; (h) That the claim or demand set forth in the plaintiff's pleading has been paid, waived, abandoned, or otherwise extinguished; (i) That the claim on which the action is founded is unenforceable under the provisions of the statute of frauds; and (j) That a condition precedent for filing the claim has not been complied with. (*Rule 16*)

A complaint should not be dismissed for insufficiency unless it appears clearly from the face of the complaint that the plaintiff is not entitled to any relief under any state of facts which could be proved within the facts alleged therein. (*GR 109173, 5 Jul 96*)

All documents attached to a complaint, the due execution and genuineness of which are not denied under oath by the defendant, must be considered as part of the complaint without need of introducing evidence thereon. The rules of procedure are not to be applied in a very rigid, technical sense; rules of procedure are used only to help secure substantial justice. If a technical and rigid enforcement of the rules is made their aim would be defeated. Where the rules are merely secondary in importance are made to override the ends of justice; the technical rules had been misapplied to the prejudice of the substantial right of a party, said rigid application cannot be countenanced. (*Ibid.*)

The proper remedy against an order denying a motion to dismiss is to file an answer and interpose as affirmative defenses the objections raised in the motion to dismiss. It is only in the presence of extraordinary circumstances evincing a patent disregard of justice and fair play where resort to a petition for certiorari is proper. (*GR 149195, 26 Jun 06*)

Before responding to a pleading, a party may move for a definite statement or for a bill of particulars of any matter which is not averred with sufficient definiteness or particularity to enable him properly to prepare his responsive pleading. Such motion shall point out the defects complained of, the paragraphs wherein they are contained, and the details desired. A bill of particulars becomes part of the pleading for which it is intended. (*Rule 12*)

Summons

Summons is a writ by which the defendant is notified of the action brought against him. Service of such writ is the means by which the court acquires jurisdiction over his person. (*GR 150636, 29 Apr 03*)

Jurisdiction over the person of the defendant in civil cases is acquired either by his voluntary appearance in court and his submission to its authority or by service of summons. (*GR 126947, 15 Jul 99*)

Well settled is the rule that summons must be served upon the defendant himself. It is only when the defendant cannot be served personally within a reasonable time that substituted service may be resorted to and such impossibility of prompt service should be shown by stating that efforts have been made to find the defendant personally and that such efforts have failed. This is necessary because substituted service is in derogation of the usual method of service. It is a method extraordinary in character and hence may be used only as prescribed and in the circumstances authorized by statute. The statutory requirements of substituted service must be followed strictly, faithfully and fully, and any substituted service other than that authorized by statute is considered ineffective. (*Ibid.*)

It should be emphasized that the service of summons is not only required to give the court jurisdiction over the person of the defendant, but also to afford the latter an opportunity to be heard on the claim made against him. Thus, compliance with the rules regarding the service of summons is as much an issue of due process as of jurisdiction. (*Ibid.*)

Fundamentally, the service of summons is intended to give official notice to the defendant or respondent that an action had been commenced against it. The defendant or respondent is thus put on guard as to the demands of the plaintiff as stated in the complaint. The service of summons, upon the defendant becomes an important element in the operation of a court's jurisdiction upon a party to a suit, as service of summons upon the defendant is the means by which the court acquires jurisdiction over his person. Without service of summons, or when summons are improperly made, both the trial and the judgment, being in violation of due process, are null and void, unless the defendant waives the service of summons by voluntarily appearing and answering the suit. (*GR 97642, 29 Aug 97*)

When a defendant voluntarily appears, he is deemed to have submitted himself to the jurisdiction of the court. This is not, however, always the case. Admittedly, and without subjecting himself to the court's jurisdiction, the defendant in an action can, by special appearance object to the court's assumption on the ground of lack of jurisdiction. If he so wishes to assert this defense, he must do so seasonably by motion for the purpose of objecting to the jurisdiction of the court, otherwise, he shall be deemed to have submitted himself to that jurisdiction. In the case of foreign corporations, it has been held that they may seek relief against the wrongful assumption of jurisdiction by local courts. (*Ibid.*)

If the defendant, besides setting up in a motion to dismiss his objections to the jurisdiction of the court, alleges at the same time any other ground for dismissing the action, or seeks an affirmative relief in the motion, he is deemed to have submitted himself to the jurisdiction of the court. (*Ibid.*)

Jurisdiction over the defendant is acquired either upon a valid service of summons or the defendant's voluntary appearance in court. When the defendant does not voluntarily submit to the court's jurisdiction or when there is no valid service of summons, "any judgment of the court which has no jurisdiction over the person of the defendant is null and void." In an action strictly *in personam*, personal service on the defendant is the preferred mode of service, that is, by handing a copy of the summons to the defendant in person. If defendant, for excusable reasons, cannot be served with the summons within a reasonable period, then substituted service can be resorted to. While substituted service of summons is permitted, "it is extraordinary in character and in derogation of the usual method of service." Hence, it must faithfully and strictly comply with the prescribed requirements and circumstances authorized by the rules. Indeed, "compliance with the rules regarding the service of summons is as much important as the issue of due process as of jurisdiction." (*GR 130974, 16 Aug 06*)

Pre-trial

The purpose of entering into a stipulation of facts or admissions of facts is to expedite trial and to relieve the parties and the court, as well, of the costs of proving facts which will not be disputed on trial and the truth of which can be ascertained by reasonable inquiry. (*GR 126802, 28 Jan 00*)

Pre-trial is a procedural device meant to limit the issues to be tackled and proved at the trial. A less cluttered case environment means that there will be fewer points of contention for the trial court to resolve. This would be in keeping with the mandate of the Constitution according every person the right to a speedy disposition of their cases. If the parties can agree on certain facts prior to trial – hence, the prefix "pre" – the court can later concentrate on those which are seemingly irreconcilable. The purpose of pre-trials is the simplification, abbreviation and expedition of the trial, if not indeed its dispensation. The stipulations are perpetuated in a pre-trial order which legally binds the parties to honor the same. (*GR 134622, 22 Oct 99*)

Pre-trial is an answer to the clarion call for the speedy disposition of cases. Hailed as "the most important procedural innovation in Anglo-Saxon justice in the nineteenth century," pre-trial seeks to achieve the following: "(a) The possibility of an amicable settlement or of a submission to alternative modes of dispute resolution; (b) The simplification of the issues; (c) The necessity or desirability of amendments to the pleadings; (d) The possibility of obtaining stipulations or admissions of facts and of documents to avoid unnecessary proof; (e) The limitation of the number of witnesses; (f) The advisability of a preliminary reference of issues to a commissioner; (g) The propriety of rendering judgment on the pleadings, or summary judgment, or of dismissing the action should a valid ground therefor be found to exist; (h) The advisability or necessity of suspending the proceedings; and (i) Such other matters as may aid in the prompt disposition of the action." (*GR 134998, 19 Jul 99*)

In light of these objectives, the parties are also required to submit a pre-trial brief, which must contain the following: "(a) A statement of their willingness to enter into amicable settlement or alternative modes of dispute resolution, indicating the desired terms thereof; (b) A summary of admitted facts and proposed stipulation of facts; (c) The issues to be tried or resolved; (d) The documents or exhibits to be presented, stating the purpose thereof; (e) A manifestation of their having availed or their intention to avail themselves of discovery procedures or referral to commissioners; and (f) The number and names of the witnesses, and the substance of their respective testimonies. (*Ibid.*)

Pre-trial is essential in the simplification and the speedy disposition of disputes. (*Ibid*)

Indeed, the pre-trial is primarily intended to make certain that all issues necessary to the disposition of a case are properly raised. The purpose is to obviate the element of surprise, hence, the parties are expected to disclose at the pre-trial conference all issues of law and fact which they intend to raise at the trial, except such as may involve privileged or impeaching matter. (*GR 130699, 12 May 00*)

Modes of Discovery

Discovery, in general, is defined as the disclosure of facts resting in the knowledge of the defendant, or as the production of deeds, writings, or things in his possession or power, in order to maintain the right or title of the party asking it, in a suit or proceeding. (*GR 97654, 14 Nov 94*)

Deposition. It is chiefly a mode of discovery, the primary function of which is to supplement the pleadings for the purpose of disclosing the real points of dispute between the parties and affording an adequate factual basis during the preparation for trial. It should be allowed absent any showing that taking it would prejudice any party. It is accorded a broad and liberal treatment and the liberty of a party to make discovery is well-nigh unrestricted if the matters inquired into are otherwise relevant and not privileged, and the inquiry is made in good faith and within the bounds of law. It is allowed as a departure from the accepted and usual judicial proceedings of examining witnesses in open court where their demeanor could be observed by the trial judge, consistent with the principle of promoting just, speedy and inexpensive disposition of every action and proceeding. (*GR163515, 31 Oct 08*)

A "deposition," in its technical and appropriate sense, is the written testimony of a witness given in the course of a judicial proceeding, in advance of the trial or hearing upon oral examination or in response to written interrogatories and where an opportunity is given for cross-examination. A deposition may be taken at any time after the institution of any action, whenever necessary or convenient. (*GR 112710, 30 May 01*)

Depositions pending action may be conducted by oral examination or written interrogatories, and may be taken at the instance of any party, with or without leave of court. (*GR 163515, supra*)

Likewise:

Under the original Rule 26 (a) of the Federal Rules of Civil Procedure, any party desiring to take depositions before answer was served was required to obtain leave of court. While the Rule did not indicate in what situations the court should grant such leave, the applicable principles are found in jurisprudence.

The general rule is that a plaintiff may not be permitted to take depositions before answer is served. Plaintiff must await joinder of issues because if the discovery is to deal with matters relevant to the case, it is difficult to know exactly what is relevant until some progress has been made toward developing the issues. Ordinarily, the issues are made up before the need for discovery arises, hence, prior to the time of delineation of the issues, the matter is in the control of the court.

There are instances, however, when a deposition is allowed to be taken before service of answer once jurisdiction has been acquired over the person or thing. Leave of court may be granted only in "exceptional" or "unusual" cases, and the decision is entirely within the discretion of the court. It should be granted only under "special circumstances" where conditions point to the necessity of presenting a strong case for allowance of the motion. There must be some "necessity" or "good reason" for taking the testimony immediately or that it would be prejudicial to the party seeking the order to be compelled to await joinder of issue. If the witness is aged or infirm, or about to leave the court's jurisdiction, or is only temporarily in the jurisdiction, leave may be granted. A general examination by deposition before answer however is premature and ordinarily not allowed, neither is mere avoidance of delay a sufficient reason. (*Ibid.*)

Interrogatories. Any party desiring to elicit material and relevant facts from any adverse parties shall file and serve upon the latter written interrogatories to be answered by the party served or, if the party served is a public or private corporation or a partnership or association, by any officer thereof competent to testify in its behalf. The interrogatories shall be answered fully in writing and shall be signed and sworn to by the person making them. The party upon whom the interrogatories have been served shall file and serve a copy of the answers on the party submitting the interrogatories within fifteen (15) days after service thereof, unless the court, on motion and for good cause shown, extends or shortens the time. Objections to any interrogatories may be presented to the court within ten (10) days after service thereof, with notice as in case of a motion; and answers shall be deferred until the objections are resolved, which shall be at as early a time as is practicable.

Admission by adverse party. At any time after issues have been joined, a party may file and serve upon any other party a written request for the admission by the latter of the genuineness of any material and relevant document described in and exhibited with the request or of the truth of any material and relevant matter of fact set forth in the request. Copies of the documents shall be delivered with the request unless copies have already been furnished. (*Rule 26*)

A party should not be compelled to admit matters of fact already admitted by his pleading and concerning which there is no issue (*Sherr vs. East, 71 A2d, 752, Terry 260, cited in 27 C.J.S. 91*), nor should he be required to make a second denial of those already denied in his answer to the complaint. A request for admission is not intended to merely reproduce or reiterate the allegations of the requesting party's pleading but should set forth relevant evidentiary matters of fact, or documents described in and exhibited with the request, whose purpose is to establish said party's cause of action or defense. Unless it serves that purpose, it is, as correctly observed by the Court of Appeals, "pointless, useless," and "a mere redundancy." (*GR 102404, 1 Feb 02*)

Production or inspection of documents or things. Rule aims to enable the parties to inform themselves, even before the trial, of all the facts relevant to the action, including those known only to the other litigants. Through this procedure, "civil trials should not be carried on in the dark." (*GR 135874, 25 Jan 00*)

It is clear that courts are given wide latitude in granting motions for discovery in order to enable parties to prepare for trial or otherwise to settle the controversy prior thereto. (*Ibid.*)

Physical and mental examination of persons. In an action in which the mental or physical condition of a party is in controversy, the court in which the action is pending may in its discretion order him to submit to a physical or mental examination by a physician. The order for examination may be made only on motion for good cause shown and upon notice to the party to be examined and to all other parties, and shall specify the time, place, manner, conditions and scope of the examination and the person or persons by whom it is to be made. If requested by the party examined, the party causing the examination to be made shall deliver to him a copy of a detailed written report of the examining physician setting out his findings and conclusions. After such request and delivery, the party causing the examination to be made shall be entitled upon request to receive from the party examined a like report of any examination, previously or thereafter made, of the same mental or physical condition. If the party examined refuses to deliver such report, the court on motion and notice may make an order requiring delivery on such terms as are just, and if a physician fails or refuses to make such a report the court may exclude his testimony if offered at the trial. By requesting and obtaining a report of the examination so ordered or by taking the deposition of the examiner, the party examined waives any privilege he may have in that action or any other involving the same controversy, regarding the testimony of every other person who has examined or may thereafter examine him in respect of the same mental or physical examination. (*Rule 28*)

Trial

As defined in Black's Law Dictionary, the term "trial" means a "judicial examination and determination of issues between parties to an action". On the other hand, the term "hearing" is "frequently used in a broader and more popular significance to describe whatever takes place before magistrates clothed with judicial functions," "at any stage of the proceedings subsequent to its inception". (*GR 128230, 13 Oct 00*)

The judge of the court where the case is pending shall personally receive the evidence to be adduced by the parties. However, in default or *ex parte* hearings, and in any case where the parties agree in writing, the court may delegate the reception of evidence to its clerk of court who is a member of the bar. The parties to any action may agree, in writing, upon the facts involved in the litigation, and submit the case for judgment on the facts agreed upon, without the introduction of evidence. (*Rule 30*)

When actions involving a common question of law or fact are pending before the court, it may order a joint hearing or trial of any or all the matters in issue in the actions; it may order all the actions consolidated; and it may make such orders concerning proceedings therein as may tend to avoid unnecessary costs or delay. The court, in furtherance of convenience or to avoid prejudice, may order a separate trial of any claim, cross-claim, counterclaim, or third-party complaint, or of any separate issue or of any number of claims, cross-claims, counterclaims, third-party complaint or issues. (*Rule 31*)

By written consent of both parties, the court may order any or all of the issues in a case to be referred to a commissioner to be agreed upon by the parties or to be appointed by the court. The word "commissioner" includes a referee, an auditor and an examiner. (*Rule 32*)

A formal trial-type hearing is not at all times and in all instances essential to due process. It is enough that the parties are given a fair and reasonable opportunity to explain their respective sides of the controversy and to present evidence on which a fair decision can be based. Due process as a constitutional precept does not, always and in all situations, require a trial-type proceedings. The essence of due process is to be found in the reasonable opportunity to be heard and to submit any evidence one may have in support of one's defense. *"To be heard"* does not only mean verbal arguments in court. One may also be heard through pleadings where opportunity to be heard, either through oral arguments or pleadings, is accorded, there is no denial of due process. (*GR 129958, 25 Nov 99*)

A motion for continuance or postponement is not a matter of right. It is addressed to the sound discretion of the Court. Action thereon will not be disturbed by appellate courts, in the absence of clear and manifest abuse of discretion resulting in a denial of substantial justice. (*GR 122539, 4 Mar 99*)

Motions for postponement are generally frowned upon by Courts if there is evidence of bad faith, malice or inexcusable negligence on the part of the movant. The inadvertence of the defense counsel in failing to take note of the trial dates and in belatedly informing the trial court of any conflict in his schedules of trial or court appearances, constitutes inexcusable negligence. It should be borne in mind that a client is bound by his counsel's conduct, negligence and mistakes in handling the case. (*Ibid.*)

Chapter 4
Dispositions

In civil cases, the burden of proof is on the plaintiff to establish his case by preponderance of evidence. "Preponderance of evidence" means evidence which is of greater weight, or more convincing than that which is offered in opposition to it. It is, therefore, premature to speak of "preponderance of evidence" in a demurrer to evidence because it is filed before the defendant presents his evidence. The purpose of a demurrer to evidence is precisely to expeditiously terminate the case without the need of the defendant's evidence. It authorizes a judgment on the merits of the case without the defendant having to submit evidence on his part as he would ordinarily have to do, if it is shown by plaintiff's evidence that the latter is not entitled to the relief sought. (*GR 161304, 27 Jul 07*)

A demurrer to evidence may be issued when, upon the facts and the law, the plaintiff has shown no right to relief. Where the plaintiff's evidence together with such inferences and conclusions as may reasonably be drawn therefrom does not warrant recovery against the defendant, a demurrer to evidence should be sustained. A demurrer to evidence is likewise sustainable when, admitting every proven fact favorable to the plaintiff and indulging in his favor all conclusions fairly and reasonably inferable therefrom, the plaintiff has failed to make out one or more of the material elements of his case, or when there is no evidence to support an allegation necessary to his claim. It should be sustained where the plaintiff's evidence is prima facie insufficient for a recovery. (*Ibid.*)

The term decision has been defined as "the adjudication or settlement of a controversy." (*L-20383, 24 May 67*). As used in the Rules of Court and in the Constitution, the words "judgments" and "decisions" have the same meaning, or at least no substantial difference between the two words is indicated. (*56 O.G. 1941*)

Summary judgment is a procedural device resorted to in order to avoid long drawn out litigations and useless delays. When the pleadings on file show that there are no genuine issues of fact to be tried, the Rules of Court allows a party to obtain immediate relief by way of summary judgment. That is, when the facts are not in dispute, the court is allowed to decide the case summarily by applying the law to the material facts. (*GR 120010, 3 Oct 02*)

Summary or accelerated judgment is a procedural technique aimed at weeding out sham claims or defenses at an early stage of the litigation, thereby avoiding the expense and loss of time involved in a trial. Even if the pleadings appear, on their face, to raise issues, summary judgment may still ensue as a matter of law if the affidavits, depositions and admissions show that such issues are not genuine. The presence or absence of a genuine issue as to any material fact determines, at bottom, the propriety of summary judgment. (*GR 175176, 17 Oct 08*)

For a summary judgment to be proper, the movant must establish two requisites: (a) there must be no genuine issue as to any material fact, except for the amount of damages; and (b) the party presenting the motion for summary judgment must be entitled to a judgment as a matter of law. Where, on the basis of the pleadings of a moving party, including documents appended thereto, no genuine issue as to a material fact exists, the burden to produce a genuine issue shifts to the opposing party. If the opposing party fails, the moving party is entitled to a summary judgment. (*Ibid.*)

A "genuine issue" is an issue of fact which requires the presentation of evidence as distinguished from a sham, fictitious, contrived or false claim. When the facts as pleaded appear uncontested or undisputed, then there is no real or genuine issue or question as to the facts, and summary judgment is called for. The party who moves for summary judgment has the burden of demonstrating clearly the absence of any genuine issue of fact, or that the issue posed in the complaint is patently unsubstantial so as not to constitute a genuine issue for trial. Trial courts have limited authority to render summary judgments and may do so only when there is clearly no genuine issue as to any material fact. When the facts as pleaded by the parties are disputed or contested, proceedings for summary judgment cannot take the place of trial. (*Ibid.*)

A decision that has acquired finality becomes immutable and unalterable, and may no longer be modified in any respect even if the modification is meant to correct erroneous conclusions of fact or law, and whether it will be made by the court that rendered it or by the highest court of the land. The reason for this is that litigation must end and terminate sometime and somewhere; and it is essential for the effective and efficient administration of justice that, once a judgment has become final, the winning party be not deprived of the fruits of the verdict. Courts must guard against any scheme calculated to bring about that result and frown upon any attempt to prolong the controversies. The only exceptions to the general rule are the correction of clerical errors, the so-called *nunc pro tunc* entries which cause no prejudice to any party, void judgments, and whenever circumstances transpire after the finality of the decision rendering its execution unjust and inequitable. (*GR 172053, 6 Oct 08*)

Nothing is more settled in law than that once a judgment attains finality it thereby becomes immutable and unalterable. It may no longer be modified in any respect, even if the modification is meant to correct what is perceived to be an erroneous conclusion of fact or law, and regardless of whether the modification is attempted to be made by the court rendering it or by the highest court of the land. Just as the losing party has the right to file an appeal within the prescribed period, the winning party also has the correlative right to enjoy the finality of the resolution of his case. The doctrine of finality of judgment is grounded on fundamental considerations of public policy and sound practice, and that, at the risk of occasional errors, the judgments or orders of courts must become final at some definite time fixed by law; otherwise, there would be no end to litigations, thus setting to naught the main role of courts of justice which is to assist in the enforcement of the rule of law and the maintenance of peace and order by settling justiciable controversies with finality. (*GR 136228, 30 Jan 01*)

A "final order" issued by a court has been defined as one which disposes of the subject matter in its entirety or terminates a particular proceeding or action, leaving nothing else to be done but to enforce by execution what has been determined by the court. As distinguished therefrom, an "interlocutory order" is one which does not dispose of a case completely, but leaves something more to be adjudicated upon. (*GR 132624, 13 Mar 00*)

A compromise agreement is a contract whereby the parties, by making reciprocal concessions, avoid a litigation or put an end to one already commenced. It contemplates mutual concessions and mutual gains to avoid the expenses of litigation, or when litigation has already begun, to end it because of uncertainty of the result. The process of compromise has long been allowed in our jurisdiction, and in the jurisdiction of other states as well. The validity of the agreement is determined by compliance with the requisites and principles of contracts. Like any other contract, the terms and conditions of a compromise agreement must not be contrary to law, morals, good customs, public policy and public order. (*GR 182421, 6 Oct 08*)

Aptly, it is also described as an agreement between two or more persons, who, for the purpose of preventing or putting an end to a lawsuit, adjust their difficulties by mutual consent in the manner which they agree on, and which each party prefers over the hope of gaining but balanced by the danger of losing. The compromise may thus be either extrajudicial (to avoid a litigation) or judicial (to put to an end a litigation). (*GR 126745, 26 Jul 99*)

Thus:

Like any other contract, an extrajudicial compromise agreement is not excepted from rules and principles of a contract. It is a consensual contract, perfected by mere consent, the latter being manifested by the meeting of the offer and the acceptance upon the thing and the cause which are to constitute the contract. It may be either perfectly valid or defective if it suffers from any impediment that, depending on the nature of its flaw, could render it void, unenforceable, voidable or rescissible.

A compromise agreement that is basically intended to resolve a matter already under litigation is what would normally be termed a judicial compromise. Once stamped with judicial *imprimatur,* it becomes more than a mere contract binding upon the parties; having the sanction of the court and entered as its determination of the controversy, it has the force and effect of any other judgment. It has the effect and authority of *res judicata,* although no execution may issue until it would have received the corresponding approval of the court where the litigation pends and its compliance with the terms of the agreement is thereupon decreed. A judicial compromise is likewise circumscribed by the rules of procedure.

Adjective law governing judicial compromises annunciate that once approved by the court, a judicial compromise is not appealable and it thereby becomes immediately executory but this rule must be understood to refer an apply only to those who are bound by the compromise and, on the assumption that they are the only parties to the case, the litigation comes to an end except only as regards to its compliance and the fulfillment by the parties of their respective obligations thereunder. The reason for the rule is that when both parties so enter into the agreement to put to a close a pending litigation between them and ask that a decision be rendered in conformity therewith, it would only be "natural to presume that such action constitutes an implicit waiver of the right to appeal" against that decision.The order approving a compromise agreement thus becomes a final act, and it forms part and parcel of the judgment that can be enforced by a writ of execution unless otherwise enjoined by a restraining order. (*Ibid.*)

An existing final judgment or decree -- rendered upon the merits, without fraud or collusion, by a court of competent jurisdiction acting upon a matter within its authority -- is conclusive of the rights of the parties and their privies. This ruling holds in all other actions or suits, in the same or any other judicial tribunal of concurrent jurisdiction, touching on the points or matters in issue in the first suit. (*GR 139020, 11 Oct 00*)

Thus:

Indeed, nothing decided on in the first appeal, between the same parties and the same facts, can be reexamined in a second or subsequent appeal. Right or wrong, the decision in the first appeal is binding on both the trial and the appellate courts for the purpose of that case and for that case only.

Courts will simply refuse to reopen what has been decided. They will not allow the same parties or their privies to litigate anew a question, once it has been considered and decided with finality. Litigations must end and terminate sometime and somewhere. The effective and efficient administration of justice requires that once a judgment has become final, the prevailing party should not be deprived of the fruits of the verdict by subsequent suits on the same issues filed by the same parties.

Courts are duty-bound to put an end to controversies. Any attempt to prolong, resurrect or juggle them should be firmly struck down. The system of judicial review should not be misused and abused to evade the operation of final and executory judgments. (*Ibid.*)

Execution of judgment

It is a settled rule that a judgment which has acquired finality becomes immutable and unalterable, hence may no longer be modified in any respect except only to correct clerical errors or mistakes. Once a judgment becomes final, all the issues between the parties are deemed resolved and laid to rest. Litigation must end and terminate sometime and somewhere, and it is essential to an effective and efficient administration of justice that, once a judgment has become final, the winning party be not deprived of the fruits of the verdict. (*GR 132250, 11 Mar 99*)

Execution of a judgment is the fruit and end of the suit, and is the life of the law. To frustrate it for several years by means of deception and dilatory schemes on the part of the losing litigants is to frustrate all the efforts, time and expenditure of the courts. (*GR 176276, 28 Nov 08*)

Execution is the final stage of litigation, the end of the suit. It can not be frustrated except for serious reasons demanded by justice and equity. In this jurisdiction, the rule is that when a judgment becomes final and executory, it is the ministerial duty of the court to issue a writ of execution to enforce the judgment. A writ of execution may however be refused on equitable grounds as when there was a change in the situation of the parties that would make execution inequitable or when certain circumstances, which transpired after judgment became final, rendered execution of judgment unjust. The fact that the decision has become final does not preclude a modification or an alteration thereof because even with the finality of judgment, when its execution becomes impossible or unjust, it may be modified or altered to harmonize the same with justice and the facts. (*GR 107014, 12 Apr 00*)

Execution is a remedy afforded by law for the enforcement of a judgment, its object being to obtain satisfaction of the judgment on which the writ is issued. It issues by order of the court *a quo*, on motion of the judgment obligee, upon finality of a judgment or order sought to be enforced, and is directed to an officer authorizing and requiring him to execute the judgment of the court. (*GR 129713, 15 Dec 99*)

Thus:

In executing a money judgment against the property of the judgment debtor, the sheriff shall levy on all property belonging to the judgment debtor as is amply sufficient to satisfy the judgment and costs, and sell the same paying to the judgment creditor so much of the proceeds as will satisfy the amount of the judgment debt and costs. Any excess in the proceeds shall be delivered to the judgment debtor unless otherwise directed by the judgment or order of the court.

Levy means the essential act or acts by which an officer sets apart or appropriates a part or the whole of the property of the judgment debtor for purposes of the prospective execution sale. The object of a levy is to take property into the custody of the law, and thereby renders it liable to the lien of the execution, and put it out of the power of the judgment debtor to divert it to any other use or purpose. A valid levy on execution places the property subject of execution under the jurisdiction and authority of the court. It also creates a lien in favor of the judgment creditor over the right, title and interest of the judgment debtor in such property at the time of the levy, subject to liens and encumbrances then existing.

A lawful levy on execution is indispensable to a valid sale on execution. In other words, a sale, unless preceded by a valid levy, is void, and the purchaser acquires no title to the property sold. Without a proper levy, the property is not placed under the authority of the court. The court does not acquire jurisdiction over the property subject of execution, hence, it could not transmit title thereto at the time of the sale. Where in the instant case no jurisdiction was acquired over the subject property, the execution sale was void and of no legal effect. And the trial court did not err in so ruling. (*Ibid.*)

The garnishment of property operates as an attachment and fastens upon the property a lien by which the property is brought under the jurisdiction of the court issuing the writ. It is brought into *custodia legis,* under the sole control of such court. A court which has control of such property, exercises exclusive jurisdiction over the same, retains all incidents relative to the conduct of such property. No court, except one having supervisory control or superior jurisdiction in the premises, has a right to interfere with and change that possession. (*GR 126731, 11 Jul 02*)

Garnishment is a species of attachment or execution for reaching any property pertaining to a judgment debtor which may be found owing to such debtor by a third person. It cites some stranger to the litigation who is debtor to one of the parties to the action. Such debtor stranger becomes a forced intervenor, and the court, having acquired jurisdiction over his person by means of citation, requires him to pay his debt, not to his former creditor, but to the new creditor, who is creditor in the main litigation. It is merely a case of involuntary novation by the substitution of one creditor for another. (*GR 161647, 22 Jun 06*)

Garnishment involves at least three (3) persons: the judgment creditor, the judgment debtor, and the garnishee, or the person cited who in turn is supposed to be indebted to the judgment creditor. (*Ibid.*)

Chapter 5
Remedies and Aspects of Procedural Recourse

Appeal

Appeal is an essential part of our judicial system. Its purpose is to bring up for review a final judgment of the lower court. (*GR 114282, 28 Nov 95*).

Basic is the rule that the perfection of an appeal within the statutory or reglementary period is not only mandatory but also jurisdictional and failure to do so renders the questioned decision final and executory, and deprives the appellate court or body of jurisdiction to alter the final judgment much less to entertain the appeal. (*GR 144678, 1 Mar 01*)

Appeal may be on questions of fact, mixed questions of fact and law or only on questions of law. (*GR 155488, 6 Dec 06*)

A question of law arises when there is doubt as to what the law is on a certain state of facts, while there is a question of fact when the doubt arises as to the truth or falsity of the alleged facts. For a question to be one of law, the same must not involve an examination of the probative value of the evidence presented by the litigants or any of them. The resolution of the issue must rest solely on what the law provides on the given set of circumstances. Once it is clear that the issue invites a review of the evidence presented, the question posed is one of fact.

Thus, the test of whether a question is one of law or of fact is not the appellation given to such question by the party raising the same; rather, it is whether the appellate court can determine the issue raised without reviewing or evaluating the evidence, in which case, it is a question of law; otherwise it is a question of fact. (*Ibid.*)

Attachment

The attachment is a mere provisional remedy to ensure the safety and preservation of the thing attached until the plaintiff can, by appropriate proceedings, obtain a judgment and have such property applied to its satisfaction. (*GR 139941, 19 Jan 01*)

For a writ of attachment to issue, the applicant must sufficiently show the factual circumstances of the alleged fraud because fraudulent intent cannot be inferred from the debtor's mere non-payment of the debt or failure to comply with his obligation. The applicant must then be able to demonstrate that the debtor has intended to defraud the creditor. (*GR 171124, 13 Feb 08*)

Thus:

To sustain an attachment on this ground, it must be shown that the debtor in contracting the debt or incurring the obligation intended to defraud the creditor. The fraud must relate to the execution of the agreement and must have been the reason which induced the other party into giving consent which he would not have otherwise given. Fraud should be committed upon contracting the obligation sued upon. A debt is fraudulently contracted if at the time of contracting it the debtor has a preconceived plan or intention not to pay, as it is in this case. Fraud is a state of mind and need not be proved by direct evidence but may be inferred from the circumstances attendant in each case.

The affidavit, being the foundation of the writ, must contain such particulars as to how the fraud imputed to respondent was committed for the court to decide whether or not to issue the writ. Absent any statement of other factual circumstances to show that respondent, at the time of contracting the obligation, had a preconceived plan or intention not to pay, or without any showing of how respondent committed the alleged fraud, the general averment in the affidavit is insufficient to support the issuance of a writ of preliminary attachment. In the application for the writ under the said ground, compelling is the need to give a hint about what constituted the fraud and how it was perpetrated because established is the rule that fraud is never presumed.

Let it be stressed that the provisional remedy of preliminary attachment is harsh and rigorous for it exposes the debtor to humiliation and annoyance. The rules governing its issuance are, therefore, strictly construed against the applicant, such that if the requisites for its grant are not shown to be all present, the court shall refrain from issuing it.

Preliminary Injunction

A preliminary injunction is an order granted at any stage of an action prior to final judgment, requiring a person to refrain from a particular act. It may be granted at any time after the commencement of the action and before final judgment, when it is established that the plaintiff is entitled to the relief demanded, and the whole or part of such relief consists in restraining the commission or continuance of the acts complained of, or in the performance of an act or acts, either for a limited period or perpetually; that the commission or continuance of some act complained of during the litigation or the non-performance thereof would probably work injustice to the plaintiff; or that the defendant is doing, threatens, or is about to do, or is procuring or suffering to be done, some act probably in violation of the plaintiff's rights respecting the subject of the action, and tending to render the judgment ineffectual. (*GR 119769, 18 Sep 96*)

A preliminary injunction, as the term itself suggests, is merely temporary, subject to the final disposition of the principal action and its purpose is to preserve the status *quo* of the things subject of the action and/or the relation between the parties, in order to protect the right of the plaintiff respecting the subject of the action during the pendency of the suit. Otherwise or if no preliminary injunction were issued, the defendant may, before final judgment, do or continue the doing of the act which the plaintiff asks the court to restrain, and thus make ineffectual the final judgment rendered afterwards granting the relief sought by the plaintiff. Its issuance rests entirely within the discretion of the court taking cognizance of the case and is generally not interfered with except in cases of manifest abuse. (*Ibid.*)

Furthermore:
In particular, for a writ of preliminary injunction to issue, the existence of the right and the violation must appear in the allegations of the complaint. A preliminary injunction is proper only when the plaintiff appears to be entitled to the relief demanded in his complaint. Moreover, injunction, like other equitable remedies, will issue only at the instance of a suitor who has sufficient interest or title in the right or property sought to be protected. Hence, for the court to act, there must be an existing basis of facts affording a present right which is directly threatened by an act sought to be enjoined. And while a clear showing of the right claimed is necessary, its existence need not be conclusively established. In fact, the evidence to be submitted to justify preliminary injunction at the hearing thereon need not be conclusive or complete but need only be a "sampling" intended merely to give the court an idea of the justification for the preliminary injunction pending the decision of the case on the merits. This should really be so since our concern here involves only the proprietary of the preliminary injunction and not the merits of the case still pending with the trial court. (*Ibid.*)

As a rule, injunction is not granted to take property out of the possession or control of one party to be placed into that of another whose title has not been clearly established by law. For the issuance of the writ of preliminary injunction to be proper, it must be shown that the invasion of the right sought to be protected is material and substantial, *that the right of complainant is clear and unmistakable* and that there is an urgent and paramount necessity for the writ to prevent serious damage. (*GR 122089, 23 Aug 00*)

Additionally, it should be stressed that the remedy of injunction could no longer be availed of where the act to be prevented had long been consummated. (*Ibid.*)

The well-settled principle is that injunctions, as a rule, will not be granted to take property out of the possession or control of one party and place it into that of another whose title has not been clearly established by law. (*GR 134343, 30 Jan 01*)

As therein likewise held:

Injunctions, like other equitable remedies, will issue only at the instance of a suitor who has sufficient interest or title in the right or property sought to be protected. It is always a ground for denying injunction that the party seeking it has insufficient title or interest to sustain it, and no claim to the ultimate relief sought – in other words, that he shows no equity. The complainant's right or title, moreover, must be clear and unquestioned, for equity, as a rule, will not lend its preventive aid by injunction where the complainant's title or right is doubtful or disputed.

To hold otherwise would be to render practically of no effect the ordinary actions, and the enforcement of judgment in such action. If a complainant could secure relief by injunction in every case where the defendant is doing or threatens or is about to do, or is procuring or suffering to be done, some act probably in violation of the plaintiff's rights and could enforce the judgment granting the injunction by the summary contempt proceedings xxx he would seldom elect to enforce his rights in such cases by the ordinary remedies, involving as they do the difficulty and oftentimes fruitless labor of enforcing judgments obtained therein by execution. (*Ibid.*)

Receivership

A receiver is a representative of the court appointing him for the purpose of preserving and conserving the property under receivership and preventing its possible destruction or dissipation, if it goes to the possession of another person. (*GR 70528-35, 14 Jul 95*). The appointment of a receiver is not a matter of absolute right. It depends upon the sound discretion of the court and is based on facts and circumstances of each particular case. (*GR 125008, 19 Jun 97*)

Thus:

The property or fund which is the subject of the action must be in danger of loss, removal or material injury which necessitates protection or preservation. The guiding principle is the prevention of imminent danger to the property. If an action by its nature, does not require such protection or preservation, said remedy cannot be applied for and granted. The "drastic sanctions" that may be brought against petitioners due to their inability to pay their employees and creditors as a result of "the numbing manner by which [respondent bank] took the ice plant" does not concern the ice plant itself. These claims are the personal liabilities of petitioners themselves. They do not constitute "material injury" to the ice plant.

The general rule is that neither party to a litigation should be appointed as receiver without the consent of the other because a receiver should be a person indifferent to the parties and should be impartial and disinterested. The receiver is not the representative of any of the parties but of all of them to the end that their interests may be equally protected with the least possible inconvenience and expense. It is only when the circumstances so demand, either because there is imminent danger that the property sought to be placed in the hands of a receiver be lost or because they run the risk of being impaired, endeavouring to avoid that the injury thereby caused be greater than the one sought to be avoided. (*Ibid.*)

Replevin

Replevin, broadly understood, is both a form of principal remedy and of a provisional relief. It may refer either to the action itself, i.e., to regain the possession of personal chattels being wrongfully detained from the plaintiff by another, or to the provisional remedy that would allow the plaintiff to retain the thing during the pendency of the action and hold it *pendente lite.* The action is primarily possessory in nature and generally determines nothing more than the right of possession. Replevin is so usually described as a mixed action, being partly *in rem* and partly *in personam-in rem* insofar as the recovery of specific property is concerned, and *in personam* as regards to damages involved. As an "action in rem," the gist of the replevin action is the right of the plaintiff to obtain possession of specific personal property by reason of his being the owner or of his having a special interest therein. Consequently, the person in possession of the property sought to be replevied is ordinarily the proper and only necessary party defendant, and the plaintiff is not required to so join as defendants other persons claiming a right on the property but not in possession thereof. (*GR 102998, 5 Jul 96*)

Hence:

Where the right of the plaintiff to the possession of the specific property is so conceded or evident, the action need only be maintained against him who so possesses the property. *In rem actio est per quam rem nostram quae ab alio possidetur petimus, et semper adversus eum est qui rem possidet.* There can be no question that persons having a special right of property in the goods the recovery of which is sought, such as a chattel mortgagee, may maintain an action for replevin therefor. Where the mortgage authorizes the mortgagee to take possession of the property on default, he may maintain an action to recover possession of the mortgaged chattels from the mortgagor or from any person in whose hands he may find them. *(Ibid.)*

Interpleader

Whenever conflicting claims upon the same subject matter are or may be made against a person who claims no interest whatever in the subject matter, or an interest which in whole or in part is not disputed by the claimants, he may bring an action against the conflicting claimants to compel them to interplead and litigate their several claims among themselves. (*Rule 62*)

It should be remembered that an action of interpleader is afforded to protect a person not against double liability but against double vexation in respect of one liability. It requires, as an indispensable requisite, that "conflicting claims upon the same subject matter are or may be made against the plaintiff-in-interpleader who claims no interest whatever in the subject matter or an interest which in whole or in part is not disputed by the claimants." (*GR 127913, 13 Sep 01*)

The resolution of the interpleader case necessitates a determination of whether the other pending cases relied upon by the trial court in dismissing the former case involves the same matters covered by the latter cases. There is a need to determine whether the pending civil cases arise out of the same facts and circumstances as those involved in the interpleader case. (*GR 120060, 9 Mar 00*)

Declaratory relief

Declaratory relief is defined as an action by any person interested in a deed, will, contract or other written instrument, executive order or resolution, to determine any question of construction or validity arising from the instrument, executive order or regulation, or statute, and for a declaration of his rights and duties thereunder. The only issue that may be raised in such a petition is the question of construction or validity of provisions in an instrument or statute. Corollary is the general rule that such an action must be justified, as no other adequate relief or remedy is available under the circumstances. (*GR 150806, 28 Jan 08*)

Decisional law enumerates the requisites of an action for declaratory relief, as follows: 1) the subject matter of the controversy must be a deed, will, contract or other written instrument, statute, executive order or regulation, or ordinance; 2) the terms of said documents and the validity thereof are doubtful and require judicial construction; 3) there must have been no breach of the documents in question; 4) there must be an actual justiciable controversy or the "ripening seeds" of one between persons whose interests are adverse; 5) the issue must be ripe for judicial determination; and 6) adequate relief is not available through other means or other forms of action or proceeding. (*Ibid.*)

The purpose of an action for declaratory relief is to secure an authoritative statement of the rights and obligations of the parties under a statute, deed, contract etc. for their guidance in the enforcement thereof, or compliance therewith, and not to settle issues arising from an alleged breach thereof. It may be entertained only before the breach or violation of the statute, deed, contract etc., to which it refers. The petition gives a practical remedy in ending controversies which have not reached the stage where other relief is immediately available. It supplies the need for a form of action that will set controversies at rest before they lead to repudiation of obligations, invasion of rights, and the commission of wrongs. (*GR 101783, 23 Jan 02*)

The remedy of reformation of an instrument is grounded on the principle of equity where, in order to express the true intention of the contracting parties, an instrument already executed is allowed by law to be reformed. The right of reformation is necessarily an invasion or limitation of the parol evidence rule since, when a writing is reformed, the result is that an oral agreement is by court decree made legally effective. Consequently, the courts, as the agencies authorized by law to exercise the power to reform an instrument, must necessarily exercise that power sparingly and with great caution and zealous care. Moreover, the remedy, being an extraordinary one, must be subject to limitations as may be provided by law. (*GR 128991, 12 Apr 00*)

Since the purpose of an action for declaratory relief is to secure an authoritative statement of the rights and obligations of the parties for their guidance in the enforcement thereof, or compliance therewith, and not to settle issues arising from an alleged breach thereof, it may be entertained only before the breach or violation of the law or contract to which it refers. (*Ibid.*)

An action for declaratory relief should be filed by a person interested under a deed, will, contract or other written instrument, and whose rights are affected by a statute, executive order, regulation or ordinance *before* breach or violation thereof. The purpose of the action is to secure an authoritative statement of the rights and obligations of the parties under a statute, deed, contract, *etc.* for their guidance in its enforcement or compliance and not to settle issues arising from its alleged breach. It may be entertained only before the breach or violation of the statute, deed, contract, *etc.* to which it refers. Where the law or contract has already been contravened prior to the filing of an action for declaratory relief, the court can no longer assume jurisdiction over the action. In other words, a court has no more jurisdiction over an action for declaratory relief if its subject, *i.e.*, the statute, deed, contract, *etc.*, has already been infringed or transgressed before the institution of the action. Under such circumstances, inasmuch as a cause of action has already accrued in favor of one or the other party, there is nothing more for the court to explain or clarify short of a judgment or final order. (*GR 144101, 16 Sep 05*)

Certiorari

An error of jurisdiction is one in which the act complained of was issued by the court, officer, or quasi-judicial body without or in excess of jurisdiction, or with grave abuse of discretion which is tantamount to lack of or in excess of jurisdiction. The purpose of the remedy of *certiorari* is to annul void proceedings; prevent unlawful and oppressive exercise of legal authority; and provide for a fair and orderly administration of justice. (*GR 168394, 6 Oct 08*)

A writ of *certiorari* may be issued only for the correction of errors of jurisdiction or grave abuse of discretion amounting to lack or excess of jurisdiction. The writ cannot be used for any other purpose, as its function is limited to keeping the inferior court within the bounds of its jurisdiction. (GR 1560677, 11 Aug 04)

For *certiorari* to prosper, the following requisites must concur: (1) the writ is directed against a tribunal, a board or any officer exercising judicial or quasi-judicial functions; (2) such tribunal, board or officer has acted without or in excess of jurisdiction, or with grave abuse of discretion amounting to lack or excess of jurisdiction; and (3) there is no appeal or any plain, speedy and adequate remedy in the ordinary course of law. (*Ibid.*)

"Without jurisdiction" means that the court acted with absolute lack of authority. There is "excess of jurisdiction" when the court transcends its power or acts without any statutory authority. "Grave abuse of discretion" implies such capricious and whimsical exercise of judgment as to be equivalent to lack or excess of jurisdiction; in other words, power is exercised in an arbitrary or despotic manner by reason of passion, prejudice, or personal hostility; and such exercise is so patent or so gross as to amount to an evasion of a positive duty or to a virtual refusal either to perform the duty enjoined or to act at all in contemplation of law. (*Ibid.*)

The prerogative writ of *certiorari* does not lie to correct every controversial interlocutory order but is confined merely to questions of jurisdiction. Its function is to keep an inferior court within its jurisdiction and to relieve persons from arbitrary acts, meaning acts which courts or judges have no power or authority in law to perform. It is not designed to correct procedural errors or the court's erroneous findings and conclusions. (*GR 140904, 9 Oct 00*)

The office of the common law writ of *certiorari* is to bring before the court for inspection the record of the proceedings of an inferior tribunal in order that the superior court may determine from the face of the record whether the inferior court has exceeded its jurisdiction, or has not proceeded according to the essential requirements of the law. However, the original function and purpose of the writ have been so modified by statutes and judicial decisions. (*GR 127444, 13 Sep 00*)

In an action for *certiorari*, the inquiry should be limited only to question of jurisdiction. As a rule, *certiorari* may be issued only where it is clearly shown that there is patent and gross abuse of discretion as to amount to an evasion of positive duty or a virtual refusal to perform a duty enjoined by law, or to act at all in contemplation of law, as where the power is exercised in an arbitrary and despotic manner by reason of passion or personal hostility. By grave abuse of discretion is such capricious and whimsical exercise of judgment as is equivalent to lack of jurisdiction, and mere abuse of discretion is not enough—it must be grave. Where the court has jurisdiction over the case, even if its findings are not correct, its questioned acts would at most constitute errors of law and not abuse of discretion correctible by *certiorari*.(*GR 117512, 2 Oct 01*)

The term *grave abuse of discretion*, in its juridical sense, connotes capricious, despotic, oppressive or whimsical exercise of judgment as is equivalent to lack of jurisdiction. The abuse must be of such degree as to amount to an evasion of positive duty or a virtual refusal to perform a duty enjoined by law, as where the power is exercised in an arbitrary and capricious manner by reason of passion and hostility. The word *capricious,* usually used in tandem with the term *arbitrary,* conveys the notion of willful and unreasoning action. Thus, when seeking the corrective hand of *certiorari*, a clear showing of caprice and arbitrariness in the exercise of discretion is imperative. (*GR 176276, 28 Nov 08*)

Generally, the special civil action for *certiorari* will not lie unless the aggrieved party has no other plain, speedy and adequate remedy in the ordinary course of law, such as a timely filed motion for reconsideration, so as to allow the lower court to correct the alleged error. However, there are several exceptions where the special civil action for certiorari will lie even without the filing of a motion for reconsideration, namely: (a) where the order is a patent nullity, as where the court *a quo* has no jurisdiction; (b) where the questions raised in the *certiorari* proceeding have been duly raised and passed upon by the lower court, or are the same as those raised and passed upon in the lower court; (c) where there is an urgent necessity for the resolution of the question and any further delay would prejudice the interests of the government or the petitioner or the subject matter of the action is perishable; (d) where, under the circumstances, a motion for reconsideration would be useless;(e) where petitioner was deprived of due process and there is extreme urgency for relief; (f) where, in a criminal case, relief from an order of arrest is urgent and the granting of such relief by the trial court is improbable; (g) where the proceedings in the lower court are a nullity for lack of due process; (h) where the proceedings was *ex parte* or in which the petitioner had no opportunity to object; and (i) where the issue raised is one purely of law or where public interest is involved. (*GR 141008, 16 Jan 01*)

It must also be stressed that what is determinative of the propriety of certiorari is the danger of failure of justice without the writ, not the mere absence of all other legal remedies. Thus, even when appeal is available and is the proper remedy, a writ of *certiorari* has been allowed when the orders of the lower court were issued either in excess of or without jurisdiction. *Certiorari* may also be availed of where an appeal would be slow, inadequate and insufficient and that to strictly observe the general rule would result in a miscarriage of justice. (*GR 108634, 17 Jul 97*)

Prohibition

Prohibition or a writ of prohibition is that process by which a superior court prevents inferior courts, tribunals, officers, or persons from usurping or exercising a jurisdiction with which they have not been vested by law. As its name indicates, the writ is one that commands the person or tribunal to whom it is directed not to do something which he or she is about to do. The writ is also commonly defined as one to prevent a tribunal possessing judicial or quasi-judicial powers from exercising jurisdiction over matters not within its cognizance or exceeding its jurisdiction in matters of which it has cognizance. At common law, prohibition was a remedy used when subordinate courts and inferior tribunals assumed jurisdiction which was not properly theirs. (*GR 150270, 26 Nov 08*)

Thus:

Prohibition, at common law, was a remedy against encroachment of jurisdiction. Its office was to restrain subordinate courts and inferior judicial tribunals from extending their jurisdiction and, in adopting the remedy, the courts have almost universally preserved its original common-law nature, object and function. Thus, as a rule, its proper function is to prevent courts, or other tribunals, officers, or persons from usurping or exercising a jurisdiction with which they are not vested by law, and confine them to the exercise of those powers legally conferred. However, the function of the writ has been extended by some authorities to cover situations where, even though the lower tribunal has jurisdiction, the superior court deems it necessary and advisable to issue the writ to prevent some palpable and irremediable injustice, and, xxx the office of the remedy in some jurisdictions has been enlarged or restricted by constitutional or statutory provisions. While prohibition has been classified as an equitable remedy, it is generally referred to as a common-law remedy or writ; it is a remedy which is in nature legal, although, xxx its issuance is governed by equitable principles. (*Citations omitted*)

Prohibition is not a new concept. It is a remedy of ancient origin. It is even said that it is as old as common law itself. The concept originated in conflicts of jurisdiction between royal courts and those of the church. (*Ibid.*)

Before resorting to the remedy of prohibition, there should be "no appeal or any other plain, speedy, and adequate remedy in the ordinary course of law." Thus, jurisprudence teaches that resort to administrative remedies should be had first before judicial intervention can be availed of. Before a party is allowed to seek the intervention of the court, it is a pre-condition that he should have availed of all the means of administrative processes afforded him. Hence, if a remedy within the administrative machinery can still be resorted to by giving the administrative officer concerned every opportunity to decide on a matter that comes within his jurisdiction then such remedy should be exhausted first before court's judicial power can be sought. The premature invocation of court's intervention is fatal to one's cause of action. (*Ibid.*)

Prohibition is a preventive remedy. It seeks for a judgment ordering the defendant to desist from continuing with the commission of an act perceived to be illegal. (*GR 107040, 12 Apr 00*)

Jurisprudence has it that prohibition will give complete relief not only by preventing what remains to be done but by undoing what has been done. The Court has authority to grant any appropriate relief within the issues presented by the pleadings of the parties:

Generally, the relief granted in a prohibition proceeding is governed by the nature of the grievance proved and the situation at the time of judgment. Although the general rule is that a writ of prohibition issues only to restrain the commission of a future act, and not to undo an act already performed, where anything remains to be done by the court, prohibition will give complete relief, not only by preventing what remains to be done but by undoing what has been done. Under some statutes, the court must grant the appropriate relief whatever the proceeding is called if facts stating ground for relief are pleaded. Although prohibition is requested only as to a particular matter, the court has authority to grant any appropriate relief within the issues presented by the pleadings. If the application for prohibition is too broad, the court may mould the writ and limit it to as much as is proper to be granted. In the exercise of its jurisdiction to issue writs, the court has, as a necessary incident thereto, the power to make such incidental order as may be necessary to maintain its jurisdiction and to effectuate its final judgment. The court may retain jurisdiction of the cause to enable it to make an appropriate order in the future, even though the petition for a writ of prohibition is dismissed. (*GR 120014, 26 Nov 02*)

Mandamus

Mandamus is a special civil action available to an aggrieved party when any tribunal, corporation, board, or person unlawfully neglects the performance of an act which the law specifically enjoins as a duty resulting from an office, trust, or station, or unlawfully excludes a person from the use and enjoyment of a right or office to which that person is entitled, and there is no other plain, speedy and adequate remedy in the ordinary course of law. (*GR 106692, 1 Sep 94*)

Mandamus is a proper recourse for citizens who seek to enforce a public right and to compel the performance of a public duty, most especially when the public right involved is mandated by the

Constitution. Besides, it has long been established in this jurisdiction that the writ of mandamus is available to the accused to compel a dismissal of the case. (*GR 164953, 13 Feb 06*)

Likewise, it is established that a writ of mandamus may be issued to control the exercise of discretion when, in the performance of duty, there is undue delay that can be characterized as a grave abuse of discretion resulting in manifest injustice. (*Ibid.*)

In order that a writ of *mandamus* may aptly issue, it is essential that, on the one hand, the person petitioning for it has a clear legal right to the claim that is sought and that, on the other hand, the respondent has an imperative duty to perform that which is demanded of him. *Mandamus* will not issue to enforce a right, or to compel compliance with a duty, which is questionable or over which a substantial doubt exists. The principal function of the writ of *mandamus* is to command and to expedite, not to inquire and to adjudicate; thus, it is neither the office nor the aim of the writ to secure a legal right but to implement that which is already established. Unless the right to the relief sought is unclouded, *mandamus* will not issue. (*GR 148789, 16 Jan 03*)

Quo warranto

Quo warranto is a demand made by the state upon some individual or corporation to show by what right they exercise some franchise or privilege appertaining to the state which, according to the Constitution and laws of the land, they cannot legally exercise except by virtue of a grant or authority from the state. In other words, a petition for *quo warranto* is a proceeding to determine the right of a person to the use or exercise of a franchise or office and to oust the holder from its enjoyment, if his claim is not well-founded, or if he has forfeited his right to enjoy the privilege. (*GR 131977, 4 Feb 99*)

Further:

The action may be commenced for the Government by the Solicitor General or the fiscal against individuals who usurp a public office, against a public officer whose acts constitute a ground for the forfeiture of his office, and against an association which acts as a corporation without being legally incorporated. The action may also be instituted by an individual in his own name who claims to be entitled to the public office or position usurped or unlawfully held or exercised by another.

Where the action is filed by a private person, he must prove that he is entitled to the controverted position, otherwise respondent has a right to the undisturbed possession of the office. If the court finds for the respondent, the judgment should simply state that the respondent is entitled to the office. If, however, the court finds for the petitioner and declares the respondent guilty of usurping, intruding into, or unlawfully holding or exercising the office, judgment may be rendered xxx. (*Ibid.*)

When the defendant is found guilty of usurping, intruding into, or unlawfully holding or exercising an office, position, right, privilege, or franchise, judgment shall be rendered that such defendant be ousted and altogether excluded therefrom, and that the plaintiff or relator, as the case may be, recover his costs. Such further judgment may be rendered determining the respective rights in and to the office, position, right, privilege, or franchise of all the parties to the action as justice requires. (*Rule 66*)

If it is found that the respondent or defendant is usurping or intruding into the office, or unlawfully holding the same, the court may order: (1) The ouster and exclusion of the defendant from office; (2) The recovery of costs by plaintiff or relator; (3) The determination of the respective rights in and to the office, position, right, privilege or franchise of all the parties to the action as justice requires. The character of the judgment to be rendered in *quo warranto* rests to some extent in the discretion of the court and on the relief sought. (*GR 131977, supra*)

Ordinarily, a judgment against a public officer in regard to a public right binds his successor in office. This rule, however, is not applicable in *quo warranto* cases. A judgment in *quo warranto* does not bind the respondent's successor in office, even though such successor may trace his title to the same source. This follows from the nature of the writ of *quo warranto* itself. It is never directed to an officer as such, but always against the person--to determine whether he is constitutionally and legally authorized to perform any act in, or exercise any function of the office to which he lays claim. (*Ibid.*)

Eminent domain

The power of eminent domain is an inherent power of the State. No constitutional conferment is necessary to vest it in the State. (*GR 137569, 23 Jun 00*)

It should be stressed that the *primary* consideration in an expropriation suit is whether the government or any of its instrumentalities has complied with the requisites for the taking of private property. Hence, the courts determine the authority of the government entity, the necessity of the expropriation, and the observance of due process. In the main, the subject of an expropriation suit is the government's exercise of eminent domain, a matter that is incapable of pecuniary estimation. (*GR 138896, 20 Jun 00*)

It is only upon payment of just compensation that title over the property passes to the government. (*GR 137569, supra*)

Thus:

In Kennedy v. Indianapolis, the US Supreme Court cited several cases holding that title to property does not pass to the condemnor until just compensation had actually been made. In fact, the decisions appear to be uniformly to this effect. As early as 1838, in Rubottom v. McLure, it was held that "actual payment to the owner of the condemned property was a condition precedent to the investment of the title to the property in the State" albeit "not to the appropriation of it to public use." In Rexford v. Knight, the Court of Appeals of New York said that the construction upon the statutes was that the fee did not vest in the State until the payment of the compensation although the authority to enter upon and appropriate the land was complete prior to the payment. Kennedy further said that "both on principle and authority the rule is . . . that the right to enter on and use the property is complete, as soon as the property is actually appropriated under the authority of law for a public use, *but that the title does not pass from the owner without his consent, until just compensation has been made to him.*" (*Ibid.*)

Constitutionally, "just compensation" is the sum equivalent to the market value of the property, broadly described as the price fixed by the seller in open market in the usual and ordinary course of legal action and competition, or the fair value of the property as between the one who receives and the one who desires to sell, it being fixed at the time of the actual taking by the government. Just compensation is defined as the full and fair equivalent of the property taken from its owner by the expropriator. It has been repeatedly stressed by the Supreme Court that the true measure is not the taker's gain but the owner's loss. The word "just" is used to modify the meaning of the word "compensation" to convey the idea that the equivalent to be given for the property to be taken shall be real, substantial, full, and ample. (*GR 157206, 27 Jun 08*)

The concept of just compensation embraces not only the correct determination of the amount to be paid to the owners of the land, but also payment within a reasonable time from its taking. Without prompt payment, compensation cannot be considered "just" inasmuch as the property owner is made to suffer the consequences of being immediately deprived of his land while being made to wait for a decade or more before actually receiving the amount necessary to cope with his loss. (*Ibid.*)

The power of eminent domain is exercised by the filing of a complaint which shall join as defendants all persons owning or claiming to own, or occupying, any part of the expropriated land or interest therein. If a known owner is not joined as defendant, he is entitled to intervene in the proceeding; or if he is joined but not served with process and the proceeding is already closed before he came to know of the condemnation, he may maintain an independent suit for damages. (*GR 109234, 20 May 98*)

The defendants in an expropriation case are not limited to the owners of the property condemned. They include all other persons owning, occupying or claiming to own the property. When a parcel of land is taken by eminent domain, the owner of the fee is not necessarily the only person who is entitled to compensation. In the American jurisdiction, the term "owner" when employed in statutes relating to eminent domain to designate the persons who are to be made parties to the proceeding, refers, as is the rule in respect of those entitled to compensation, to *all those who have lawful interest in the property to be condemned*, including a mortgagee, a lessee and a vendee in possession under an executory contract. Every person having an estate or interest at law or in equity in the land taken is entitled to share in the award. If a person claiming an interest in the land sought to be condemned is not made a party, he is given the right to intervene and lay claim to the compensation. (*Ibid.*)

Contempt of court

Contempt is defined as a disobedience to the court by setting up an opposition to its authority, justice and dignity. (*AM-MTJ 9-1238, 24 Jan 03*)

The power to punish for contempt is inherent in all courts. It is indispensable to their right of self-preservation, to the execution of their powers, and to the maintenance of their authority, and consequently to the due administration of justice. It is an essential element, or is possessed as part, of judicial authority vested by the Constitution in the courts. Put a little differently, the power is an "implied constitutional power." (*GR 120654, 11 Sep 96*)

The power, however, is not limitless. It must be used sparingly with caution, restraint, judiciousness, deliberation, and due regard to the provisions of the law and the constitutional rights of the individual. It should be exercised on the preservative and not on the vindictive principle. Being drastic and extraordinary in its nature, it should not be resorted to unless necessary in the interest of justice. (*Ibid.*)

The power to declare a person in contempt of court and in dealing with him accordingly is a means to protect and preserve the dignity of the court, the solemnity of the proceedings therein and the administration of justice from callous misbehavior and offensive personalities. (*GR 117266, 13 Mar 97*)

The real character of the proceedings in contempt cases is to be determined by the relief sought or by the dominant purpose. The proceedings are to be regarded as criminal when the purpose is primarily punishment, and civil when the purpose is primarily compensatory or remedial. (*GR 107671, 26 Feb 97*)

No protection for falsehood

Contempt exists with or without a pending case, as what is sought to be protected is the court itself and its dignity. (12 Am. Jur. Pp. 416-417) Courts would lose their utility if public confidence in them is destroyed. (AM 93-2-037 SC, 6 Apr 95)

Likewise:

Advertences to lofty principle, however eloquent and enlightening, hardly address the mundane, but immediate and very pertinent, question of whether a journalist may put in print unverified information derogatory of the courts and judges and yet remain immune from liability for contempt for refusing, when called upon, to demonstrate their truth on the ground of press freedom or by simply claiming that he need not do so since (or if) it would compel him to disclose the identity of his source or sources.

True, the pre-eminent role of a free press in keeping freedom alive and democracy in full bloom cannot be overemphasized. But it is debatable if that role is well and truly filled by a press let loose to print what it will, without reasonable restraints designed to assure the truth and accuracy of what is published. The value of information to a free society is in direct proportion to the truth it contains. That value reduces to little or nothing when it is no longer possible for the public to distinguish between truth and falsehood in news reports, and the courts are denied the mechanisms by which to make reasonably sure that only the truth reaches print.

It is worth stressing that false reports about a public official or other person are not shielded from sanction by the cardinal right to free speech enshrined in the Constitution. Even the most liberal view of free speech has never countenanced the publication of falsehoods, specially the persistent and unmitigated dissemination of patent lies. The U.S. Supreme Court, while asserting that "(u)nder the First Amendment there is no such thing as a false idea," and that "(h)owever pernicious an opinion may seem, we depend for its correction not on the conscience of judges and juries but on the competition of other ideas" (citing a passage from the first Inaugural Address of Thomas Jefferson), nonetheless made the firm pronouncement that "there is no constitutional value in false statements of fact," and "the erroneous statement of fact is not worthy of constitutional protection (although) . . . nevertheless inevitable in free debate." "Neither the intentional lie nor the careless error," it said, "materially advances society's interest in "unhibited, robust, and wide-open" debate on public issues. New York Times Co. v. Sullivan, 376 US, at 270, 11 L Ed 2d 686, 95 ALR2d 1412. They belong to that category of utterances which "are no essential part of any exposition of ideas, and are of such slight social value as a step to the truth that any benefit that may be derived from them is clearly outweighed by the social interest in order and morality." Chaplinsky v, new Hampshire, 315 US 568, 572, 86 L Ed 1031, 62 S Ct 766 (1942). (*Ibid.*)

Habeas corpus

Habeas corpus is a writ directed to the person detaining another, commanding him to produce the body of the prisoner at a designated time and place, with the day and cause of his capture and detention, to do, submit to, and receive whatsoever the court or judge awarding the writ shall consider in that behalf. (*GR 139789, 139808, 12 May 00*)

The writ of *habeas corpus* extends to "all case of illegal confinement or detention by which any person is deprived of his liberty, or by which the rightful custody of any person is withheld from the person entitled thereto." The remedy of *habeas corpus* has one objective: to inquire into the cause of detention of a person, and if found illegal, the court orders the release of the detainee. If, however, the detention is proven lawful, then the *habeas corpus* proceedings terminate. *(GR 167193, 19 Apr 06)*

It is available where a person continues to be unlawfully denied of one or more of his constitutional freedoms, where there is denial of due process, where the restraints are not merely involuntary but are unnecessary, and where a deprivation of freedom originally valid has later become arbitrary. It is devised as a speedy and effectual remedy to relieve persons from unlawful restraint, as the best and only sufficient defense of personal freedom. (*GR 139789, 139808, supra*)

The essential object and purpose of the writ of *habeas corpus* is to inquire into all manner of involuntary restraint, and to relieve a person therefrom if such restraint is illegal. (*Ibid.*)

To justify the grant of the petition, the restraint of liberty must be an illegal and involuntary deprivation of freedom of action. The illegal restraint of liberty must be actual and effective, not merely nominal or moral. (*Ibid.*)

Habeas corpus may be resorted to in cases where rightful custody is withheld from a person entitled thereto. In a petition for *habeas corpus*, the child's welfare is the supreme consideration. In all questions regarding the care and custody, among others, of the child, his welfare shall be the paramount consideration. (*GR 162734, 29 Aug 06*)

Chapter 6
Appurtenances to Actions

A prior resort to a system of amicably settling disputes among family and village members without judicial recourse has been established in the Philippines as a pre-requisite to the institution of suits in the regular courts of justice. This has been institutionalized with the effectuality of the law, Republic Act No. 7160, which took effect on January 1, 1992 codifying the previously decreed practice of administering justice at the lowest level of the political hierarchy.

Prior conciliation proceedings were thus conducted to sway the parties into an amicable settlement of their disputes which positively resulted in compromise agreements arrived at by the parties.

The practice primarily benefited litigants who are residents of the same village and whose cases are not grave or serious as determined by the guidelines issued by the Chief Justice of the Philippine Supreme Court in implementation of the specific provisions of the Code (R.A. No. 7160).

Compromise

A compromise is "a contract whereby the parties, by making reciprocal concessions, avoid litigation or put an end to one already commenced." Parties to a compromise are motivated by "the hope of gaining, balanced by the dangers of losing." It contemplates mutual concessions and mutual gains to avoid the expenses of litigation, or, when litigation has already begun, to end it because of the uncertainty of the result. (*GR 166421, 5 Sep 06*)

The Labor Code of the Philippines authorizes compromise agreements voluntarily agreed upon by the parties, in conformity with the basic policy of the State "to promote and emphasize the primacy of free collective bargaining and negotiations, including voluntary arbitration, mediation and conciliation, as modes of settling labor or industrial disputes." (*Ibid.*)

A judgment rendered in accordance with a compromise agreement is not appealable, and is immediately executory unless a motion is filed to set aside the agreement on the ground of fraud, mistake, or duress, in which case an appeal may be taken against the order denying the motion. Under the Civil Code, "a compromise has upon the parties the effect and authority of *res judicata*," even when effected without judicial approval; and under the principle of *res judicata*, an issue which had already been laid to rest by the parties themselves can no longer be relitigated. (*Ibid.*)

Once stamped with judicial imprimatur, a compromise agreement becomes more than a mere contract binding upon the parties; having the sanction of the court and entered as its determination of the controversy, it has the force and effect of any other judgment. Since a judgment based on a compromise agreement is no different from any other judgment, once it attains finality, it can no longer be subject to any alteration, modification or review. (*GR 142236, 27 Sep 06*)

The orderly administration of justice requires that the judgments/resolutions of a court or quasi-judicial body must reach a point of finality set by the law, rules and regulations. The noble purpose is to write finis to disputes once and for all. This is a fundamental principle in our justice system, without which there could be no end to litigations. Utmost respect and adherence to this principle must always be maintained by those who wield the power of adjudication. Any act which violates such principle must be struck down. (*Ibid.*)

While a compromise agreement or an amicable settlement is very strongly encouraged, the failure to consummate one does not warrant any procedural sanction, much less provide an authority for the court to jettison the case. (*GR 168799, 27 Jun 08*)

Arbitral awards

The voluntary arbitrator is vested with the power and the authority to see to it that his arbitral award is fully satisfied. Thus, he may issue writs of execution requiring a sheriff or a proper officer to execute his final decisions, orders or awards and take any measure under existing laws to ensure compliance with his decisions, orders or awards. The sheriffs, tasked to implement the said writ, are not sheriffs of the ordinary court but labor sheriffs under the supervision of the voluntary arbitrator. (*GR118491, 31 Jan 96*)

Thus:

The power of the voluntary arbitrator to issue a writ of execution carries with it the power to inquire into the correctness of the execution of his decision and to consider whatever supervening event that may transpire during such execution.

Jurisprudence is replete with the rule that a case in which an execution has been issued is considered as still pending so that all proceedings on the execution are proceedings in the suit. Moreover, there is no dispute with the view that the tribunal which rendered the decision or award has a general supervisory control over the process of its execution, and this includes the power to determine every question of fact and law which may be involved in the execution. This is because any court which issued a writ of execution has the inherent power, for the advancement of justice, to correct error of its ministerial officers and to control its own processes. Hence, any irregularities which attended the execution of the decision or award brought out by the enforcement of a dead writ of execution must be litigated in the court which issued it. (*Ibid.*)

Forum shopping

Forum-shopping is an act of a party against whom an adverse judgment or order has been rendered in one forum of seeking and possibly getting a favorable opinion in another forum, other than by appeal or special civil action for certiorari. It may also be the institution of two or more actions or proceedings grounded on the same cause on the supposition that one or the other court would make a favorable disposition. For it to exist, there should be (a) identity of parties, or at least such parties as would represent the same interest in both actions; (b) identity of rights asserted and relief prayed for, the relief being founded on the same facts; and (c) identity of the two preceding particulars such that any judgment rendered in the other action will, regardless of which party is successful, amount to *res judicata* in the action under consideration. (*GR 155618, 26 Mar 03*)

Forum-shopping is considered a pernicious evil; it adversely affects the efficient administration of justice since it clogs the court dockets, unduly burdens the financial and human resources of the judiciary, and trifles with and mocks judicial processes. The most important factor in determining the existence of forum shopping is the vexation caused the courts and parties-litigants by a party who asks different courts to rule on the same or related causes or grant the same or substantially the same reliefs. (*Ibid.*)

In determining whether or not there is forum-shopping, what is important is the vexation caused the courts and parties-litigant by a party who asks different courts and/or administrative agencies to rule on the same or related causes and/or grant the same or substantially the same reliefs and in the process creating the possibility of conflicting decisions being rendered by the different fora upon the same issues. (*GR 128632, 5 Aug 99*)

A party is not permitted to "pursue simultaneous remedies in two different (fora)." This is a practice which derogates and ridicules the judicial process, plays havoc with the rules of orderly procedure, and is vexatious and unfair to the other parties to the case. Hence, forum-shopping is both contumacious and an act of malpractice; it is "proscribed and condemned as trifling with the courts and abusive of their processes (warranting) prosecution for contempt of court and (constituting) ground for summary dismissal of the actions involved, without prejudice to appropriate administrative action against the counsel." (*GR 123332, 3 Feb 97*)

The Rules of Court, the code governing judicial procedure, prescribes the remedies (actions and special proceedings) that may be availed of for the myriad reliefs that persons may conceivably have need of and seek in this jurisdiction. But that the adjective law makes available several remedies does not imply that a party may resort to them simultaneously or at his pleasure or whim. There is a sequence and a hierarchical order which must be observed in availing of them. Impatience at what may be felt to be the slowness of the judicial process, or even a deeply held persuasion in the rightness of one's cause, does not justify short-cuts in procedure, or playing fast and loose with the rules thereof. (*Ibid.*)

Withdrawal, dismissal of actions

A complaint may be dismissed by the plaintiff by filing a notice of dismissal at any time before service of the answer or of a motion for summary judgment. Upon such notice being filed, the court shall issue an order confirming the dismissal. Unless otherwise stated in the notice, the dismissal is without prejudice, except that a notice operates as an adjudication upon the merits when filed by a plaintiff who has once dismissed in a competent court an action based on or including the same claim. (*Rule 17*)

Except as provided in the preceding section, a complaint shall not be dismissed at the plaintiff's instance save upon approval of the court and upon such terms and conditions as the court deems proper. If a counterclaim has been pleaded by a defendant prior to the service upon him of the plaintiff's motion for dismissal, the dismissal shall be limited to the complaint. The dismissal shall be without prejudice to the right of the defendant to prosecute his counterclaim in a separate action unless within fifteen (15) days from notice of the motion he manifests his preference to have his counterclaim resolved in the same action. Unless otherwise specified in the order, a dismissal under this paragraph shall be without prejudice. A class suit shall not be dismissed or compromised without the approval of the court. (*Ibid.*)

If, for no justifiable cause, the plaintiff fails to appear on the date of the presentation of his evidence in chief on the complaint, or to prosecute his action for an unreasonable length of time, or to comply with these Rules or any order of the court, the complaint may be dismissed upon motion of the defendant or upon the court's own motion, without prejudice to the right of the defendant to prosecute his counterclaim in the same or in a separate action. This dismissal shall have the effect of an adjudication upon the merits, unless otherwise declared by the court. (*Ibid.*)

The expeditious disposition of cases is as much the duty of the plaintiff as the court. It must be remembered that a defendant in a case likewise has the right to the speedy disposition of the action filed against him, considering that any delay in the proceedings entails prolonged anxiety and valuable time wasted. (*GR 167403, 6 Aug 08*)

While a court can dismiss a case on the ground of *non prosequitur*, the real test of such power is whether, under the circumstances, plaintiff is chargeable with want of due diligence in failing to proceed with reasonable promptitude. In the absence of a pattern or a scheme to delay the disposition of the case or a wanton failure to observe the mandatory requirement of the rules on the part of the plaintiff, courts should decide to dispense rather than wield their authority to dismiss. (*GR 117385, 11 Feb 99*)

Once a case is dismissed for failure to prosecute, this has the effect of an adjudication on the merits and is understood to be with prejudice to the filing of another action unless otherwise provided in the order of dismissal. In other words, unless there be a qualification in the order of dismissal that it is without prejudice, the dismissal should be regarded as an adjudication on the merits and is with prejudice. (*GR 108015, 109234, 9 Oct 00*)

Part Two

Proving Your Case

Introduction

The road which the quest for the truth takes is not easy. Proof is needed in order that the truth may be arrived at. Litigation most often can be protracted and the desired verdict, even if eventually achieved, may turn out to be too little, too late.

The truth, as a consequence, needs a lot of proof, admissions and presumptions.

Evidence thus plays a significant role and although its ramifications dished out in this book are primarily based on the Philippine usage and experience, it has to be borne in mind that the tenets and precepts adhered to are almost uniform in their global application. The same practices hold true: that to arrive at the factual conclusion, there is a need for witnesses who have to be directly examined and who, thereafter, should be cross-examined. Circumstantial evidence, opinions of experts, etc. are almost universally considered and adopted as means of finding out the truth.

It is thus in the light of the foregoing that the rules and jurisprudence maintained in the Philippine setting are used as basis for this book. As to citations in the work, a *GR number* refers to the identification of the record in the set of cases decided by the Supreme Court, the highest tribunal in the judicial hierarchy of the country, with the appurtenant date when the same was promulgated. The Rule cited refers to the Revised Rules on Evidence presently being in effect and the number preceding refers to a particular rule and the number thereafter refers to a particular provision.

Chapter 7
Evidence, in general

The term "evidence" as defined in *Funk and Wagnalls Standard Desk Dictionary* refers to that which is properly presented before a court as a means of establishing or disproving something alleged or presumed, as the statements of witnesses.

Evidence is the means, sanctioned by the rules, of ascertaining in a judicial proceeding the truth respecting a matter of fact. (*128 Rule 1*)

Admissibility and Relevancy of Evidence
Evidence is admissible when it is relevant to the issue and is not excluded by the law or the rules. (*128 Rule 3*)

Evidence must have such a relation to the fact in issue as to induce belief in its existence or non-existence. Evidence on collateral matters shall not be allowed, except when it tends in any reasonable degree to establish the probability or improbability of the fact in issue. (*128 Rule 4*)

There are, however, certain matters that need not be proved. Judicial notice and judicial admissions dispense with the need for introduction of evidence.

Judicial notice, when mandatory and discretionary

A court shall take judicial notice, without the introduction of evidence, of the existence and territorial extent of states, their political history, forms of government and symbols of nationality, the law of nations, the admiralty and maritime courts of the world and their seals, the political constitution and history of the Philippines, the official acts of the legislative, executive and judicial departments of the Philippines, the laws of nature, the measure of time, and the geographical divisions.(*129 Rule 1*)

A court may take judicial notice of matters which are of public knowledge, or are capable of unquestionable demonstration, or ought to be known to judges because of their judicial functions. (*129 Rule 2*). Otherwise, the court must receive evidence of disputed facts with notice to the parties. (*GR 121099, 17 Feb 99*). Judicial notice signifies that there are certain "*facta probanda*," or propositions in a party's case, as to which he will not be required to offer evidence; these will be taken for true by the tribunal without the need of evidence. Judicial notice, however, is a phrase sometimes used in a loose way to cover some other judicial action. Certain rules of Evidence, usually known under other names, are frequently referred to in terms of judicial notice. (*GR 131516, 5 Mar 03*)

Judicial notice is the cognizance of certain facts which judges may properly take and act on without proof because they already know them. Judicial notice may either be mandatory or discretionary. (*GR 135695-96, 12 Oct 00*). Judicial cognizance is based on considerations of expediency and convenience. It displaces evidence since, being equivalent to proof, it fulfills the object which the evidence is intended to achieve. (*GR 170422, 7 Mar 08*)

The concept of "facts of common knowledge" in the context of judicial notice has been explained as those facts that are "so commonly known in the community as to make it unprofitable to require proof, and so certainly known to as to make it indisputable among reasonable men." Moreover, "though usually facts of 'common knowledge' will be generally known throughout the country, it is sufficient as a basis for judicial notice that they be known in the local community where the trial court sits." (*GR 159507, 19 Apr 06*)

When hearing is necessary

During the trial, the court, on its own initiative, or on request of a party, may announce its intention to take judicial notice of any matter and allow the parties to be heard thereon.

After the trial, and before judgment or on appeal, the proper court, on its own initiative or on request of a party, may take judicial notice of any matter and allow the parties to be heard thereon if such matter is decisive of a material issue in the case.(*129 Rule 3*)

Judicial admissions

An admission, verbal or written, made by a party in the course of the proceedings in the same case, does not require proof. The admission may be contradicted only by showing that it was made through palpable mistake or that no such admission was made. (*129 Rule 4*)

Generally, "a judicial admission is conclusive upon the party making it and does not require proof except (1) when it is made through palpable mistake and (2) when it is shown that no admission was in fact made. "In spite of the presence of judicial admission in a party's pleading, the trial court is still given leeway to consider other evidence presented." (*GR 106102, 29 Oct 99*)

The general rule that "the allegations, statements, or admissions contained in a pleading are conclusive as against the pleader" is not an absolute and inflexible rule and is subject to exceptions. In other words, an admission in a pleading on which a party goes to trial may be contradicted by showing that it was made by improvidence or mistake or that no such admission was made, i.e., "not in the sense in which the admission was made to appear or the admission was taken out of context." (*GR 74336, 7 Apr 97*)

Judicial admissions verbal or written made by the parties in the pleadings or in the course of the trial or other proceedings in the same case are conclusive, no evidence being required to prove the same and cannot be contradicted unless shown to have been made through palpable mistake or that no such admission was made. (*GR 119845, 5 Jul 96*)

A party who judicially admits a fact cannot later challenge that fact as judicial admissions are a waiver of proof; production of evidence is dispensed with. A judicial admission also removes an admitted fact from the field of controversy. Consequently, an admission made in the pleadings cannot be controverted by the party making such admission and are conclusive as to such party, and all proofs to the contrary or inconsistent therewith should be ignored, whether objection is interposed by the party or not. The allegations, statements or admissions contained in a pleading are conclusive as against the pleader. A party cannot subsequently take a position contrary of or inconsistent with what was pleaded. (*GR 165987, 31 Mar 06*)

While the admission is admissible in evidence, its probative value is to be determined from the whole statement and others intimately related or connected therewith as an integrated unit. Although acts or facts admitted do not require proof and cannot be contradicted, however, evidence *aliunde* can be presented to show that the admission was made through palpable mistake. The rule is always in favor of liberality in construction of pleadings so that the real matter in dispute may be submitted to the judgment of the court. (*GR 1235583, 13 July 98*)

Chapter 8
Physical and Documentary Evidence

Objects and Documents

Objects as evidence are those addressed to the senses of the court. When an object is relevant to the fact in issue, it may be exhibited to, examined or viewed by the court. (*130 Rule 1*) Documents as evidence consist of writings or any material containing letters, words, numbers, figures, symbols or other modes of written expressions offered as proof of their contents. (*130 Rule 2*)

Physical evidence is a mute but an eloquent manifestation of truth, and it ranks high in our hierarchy of trustworthy evidence. (GR *118441-42, 18 Jan 00*). Where the physical evidence on record runs counter to the testimony of witnesses, the primacy of the physical evidence must be upheld. (*GR119832, 12 Oct 00*)

As between a writing or document made contemporaneously with a transaction in which are evidenced facts pertinent to an issue, when admitted as proof of these facts, is ordinarily regarded as more reliable proof and of greater probative value than oral testimony of a witness as to such facts based upon memory and recollection. The reason behind this is obvious, human memory is fallible and its force diminishes with the lapse of time. Hence, as between testimony and written report, the latter is considered as the more accurate account. (*GR 114261, 10 Feb 00*)

Best evidence rule

When the subject of inquiry is the contents of a document, no evidence shall be admissible other than the original document itself, except: (a) When the original has been lost or destroyed, or cannot be produced in court, without bad faith on the part of the offeror; (b) When the original is in the custody or under the control of the party against whom the evidence is offered, and the latter fails to produce it after reasonable notice; (c) When the original consists of numerous accounts or other documents which cannot be examined in court without great loss of time and the fact sought to be established from them is only the general result of the whole; and (d) When the original is a public record in the custody of a public officer or is recorded in a public office. (*130 Rule 3*)

The "best evidence rule," according to Professor Thayer, first appeared in the year 1699-1700 when in one case involving a goldsmith, Holt, C. J., was quoted as stating that they should take into consideration the usages of trade and that "the best proof that the nature of the thing will afford is only required." Over the years, the phrase was used to describe rules which were already existing such as the rule that the terms of a document must be proved by the production of the document itself, in preference to evidence about the document; it was also utilized to designate the hearsay rule or the rule excluding assertions made out of court and not subject to the rigors of cross-examination; and the phrase was likewise used to designate the group of rules by which testimony of particular classes of witnesses was preferred to that of others. (*GR 143338, 29 Jul 05*)

According to McCormick, an authority on the rules of evidence, "the only actual rule that the 'best evidence' phrase denotes today is the rule requiring the production of the original writing" the rationale being:

(1) that precision in presenting to the court the exact words of the writing is of more than average importance, particularly as respects operative or dispositive instruments, such as deeds, wills and contracts, since a slight variation in words may mean a great difference in rights, (2) that there is a

substantial hazard of inaccuracy in the human process of making a copy by handwriting or typewriting, and (3) as respects oral testimony purporting to give from memory the terms of a writing, there is a special risk of error, greater than in the case of attempts at describing other situations generally. In the light of these dangers of mistransmission, accompanying the use of written copies or of recollection, largely avoided through proving the terms by presenting the writing itself, the preference for the original writing is justified. (*Ibid.*)

A notarial document is evidence of the facts in the clear unequivocal manner therein expressed and has in its favor the presumption of regularity. (*GR 156310, 31 Jul 208*)The original of a document is one the contents of which are the subject of inquiry. When a document is in two or more copies executed at or about the same time, with identical contents, all such copies are equally regarded as originals. When an entry is repeated in the regular course of business, one being copied from another at or near the time of the transaction, all the entries are likewise equally regarded as originals. (*130 Rule 4*)

When the original document has been lost or destroyed, or cannot be produced in court, the offeror, upon proof of its execution or existence and the cause of its unavailability without bad faith on his part, may prove its contents by a copy, or by a recital of its contents in some authentic document, or by the testimony of witnesses in the order stated. (*130 Rule 5*)

If the document is in the custody or under the control of the adverse party, he must have reasonable notice to produce it. If after such notice and after satisfactory proof of its existence, he fails to produce the document, secondary evidence may be presented as in the case of its loss. (*130 Rule 6*)

The mere fact that the original of the writing is in the custody or control of the party against whom it is offered does not warrant the admission of secondary evidence. The offeror must prove that he has done all in his power to secure the best evidence by giving notice to the said party to produce the document. The notice may be in the form of a motion for the production of the original or made in open court in the presence of the adverse party or *via* a *subpoena duces tecum*, provided that the party in custody of the original has sufficient time to produce the same. When such party has the original of the writing and does not voluntarily offer to produce it or refuses to produce it, secondary evidence may be admitted. (*GR 152881, 17 Aug 04*)

When the original of a document is in the custody of a public officer or is recorded in a public office, its contents may be proved by a certified copy issued by the public officer in custody thereof. (*130 Rule 7*)

A party who calls for the production of a document and inspects the same is not obliged to offer it as evidence. (*130 Rule 8*)

The purpose of the rule requiring the production by the offeror of the best evidence is the prevention of fraud, because if a party is in possession of such evidence and withholds it and presents inferior or secondary evidence in its place, the presumption is that the latter evidence is withheld from the court and the adverse party for a fraudulent or devious purpose which its production would expose and defeat. As long as the original evidence can be had, the court should not receive in evidence that which is substitutionary in nature, such as photocopies, in the absence of any clear showing that the original writing has been lost or destroyed or cannot be produced in court. Such photocopies must be disregarded, being inadmissible evidence and barren of probative weight. (*GR 152881, supra*)

Parol evidence rule

When the terms of an agreement have been reduced to writing, it is considered as containing all the terms agreed upon and there can be, between the parties and their successors in interest, no evidence of such terms other than the contents of the written agreement. However, a party may present evidence to modify, explain or add to the terms of the written agreement if he puts in issue in his pleading:(a) An intrinsic ambiguity, mistake or imperfection in the written agreement;(b) The failure of the written agreement to express the true intent and agreement of the parties thereto;(c) The validity of the written agreement; or (d) The existence of other terms agreed to by the parties or their successors in interest after the execution of the written agreement. The term "agreement" includes wills. (*130 Rule 9*)

The so-called "parol evidence" forbids any addition to or contradiction of the terms of a written instrument by testimony purporting to show that, at or before the signing of the document, other terms were orally agreed on by the parties.

Under the rule, the terms of the written contract are conclusive upon the parties and evidence *aliunde* is inadmissible to vary an enforceable agreement embodied in the document. However, the rule is not absolute and admits of exceptions. (*GR 171707, 28 Jul 08*)

The first exception applies when the ambiguity or uncertainty is readily apparent from reading the contract. The wordings are so defective that what the author of the document intended to say cannot be deciphered. It also covers cases where the parties commit a mutual mistake of fact, or where the document is manifestly incomplete as the parties do not intend to exhibit the whole agreement but only to define some of its terms. The second exception includes instances where the contract is so obscure that the contractual intention of the parties cannot be understood by mere inspection of the instrument. Thus, extrinsic proof of its subject matter, of the relation of the parties and of the circumstances surrounding them when they entered into the contract may be received as evidence. Under the third exception, the parol evidence rule does not apply where the purpose of introducing the evidence is to show the invalidity of the contract. This includes cases where a party alleges that no written contract ever existed, or the parties fail to agree on the terms of the contract, or there is no consideration for such agreement. The fourth exception involves a situation where the due execution of the contract or document is in issue. (*Ibid.*)

Where a party entitled to the benefit of the parol evidence rule allows such evidence to be received without objection, he cannot, after the trial has closed and the case has been decided against him, invoke the rule in order to secure a reversal of the judgment. (*Ibid.*)

Interpretation of Documents

The language of a writing is to be interpreted according to the legal meaning it bears in the place of its execution, unless the parties intended otherwise. In the construction of an instrument where there are several provisions or particulars, such a construction is, if possible, to be adopted as will give effect to all. In the construction of an instrument, the intention of the parties is to be pursued; and when a general and a particular provision are inconsistent, the latter is paramount to the former. So a particular intent will control a general one that is inconsistent with it. For the proper construction of an instrument, the circumstances under which it was made, including the situation of the subject thereof and of the parties to it, may be shown, so that the judge may be placed in the position of those whose language he is to interpret. The terms of a writing are presumed to have been used in their primary and general acceptation, but evidence is admissible to show that they have a local, technical, or otherwise peculiar signification, and were so used and understood, in the particular instance, in which case the agreement must be construed accordingly. When an instrument consists partly of written words and partly of a printed form, and the two are inconsistent, the former controls the latter. When the characters in which an instrument is written are difficult to be deciphered, or the language is not understood by the court, the evidence of persons skilled in deciphering the characters, or who understand the language, is admissible to declare the characters or the meaning of the language. When the terms of an agreement have been intended in a different sense by the different parties to it, that sense is to prevail against either party in which he supposed the other understood it, and when different constructions of a provision are otherwise equally proper, that is to be taken which is the most favorable to the party in whose favor the provision is made. When an instrument is equally susceptible of two interpretations, one in favor of natural right and the other against it, the former is to be adopted. An instrument may be construed according to usage, in order to determine its true character. (*130 Rule 10-19*)

Chapter 9
Witnesses

Testimonial Evidence

All persons who can perceive, and perceiving, can make known their perception to others, may be witnesses except as provided in the succeeding. Religious or political belief, interest in the outcome of the case, or conviction of a crime unless otherwise provided by law, shall not be a ground for disqualification. (*130 Rule 20*)

A person is qualified and competent to be a witness if—

(a) he is capable of perceiving and (b) perceiving, he can make his perception known. Unless disqualified, such a person would be capable of testifying. In consonance with the modern trend to broaden the field of competency of witnesses and to restrict that of incompetency, even a person convicted of a crime or one who has a pending criminal case is not by that alone disqualified from testifying. (GR 119332, 29 Aug 97)

The following persons cannot be witnesses: (a) Those whose mental condition, at the time of their production for examination, is such that they are incapable of intelligently making known their perception to others; (b) Children whose mental maturity is such as to render them incapable of perceiving the facts respecting which they are examined and of relating them truthfully. (*130 Rule 21*)

A mental retardate is not, *per se*, disqualified from being a witness. As long as his senses can perceive facts and if he can convey his perceptions in court, he can be a witness. To be sure, modern rules on evidence have downgraded mental incapacity as a ground to disqualify a witness. As observed by McCormick, the remedy of excluding such a witness who may be the only person available who knows the facts, seems inept and primitive. (*GR 119308, 18 Apr 97*)

During their marriage, neither the husband nor the wife may testify for or against the other without the consent of the affected spouse, except in a civil case by one against the other, or in a criminal case for a crime committed by one against the other or the latter's direct descendants or ascendants.(*130 Rule 22*)

Parties or assignors of parties to a case, or persons in whose behalf a case is prosecuted, against an executor or administrator or other representative of a deceased person, or against a person of unsound mind, upon a claim or demand against the estate of such deceased person or against such person of unsound mind, cannot testify as to any matter of fact occurring before the death of such deceased person or before such person became of unsound mind. (*130 Rule 23*)

The following persons cannot testify as to matters learned in confidence in the following cases: (a) The husband or the wife, during or after the marriage, cannot be examined without the consent of the other as to any communication received in confidence by one from the other during the marriage except in a civil case by one against the other, or in a criminal case for a crime committed by one against the other or the latter's direct descendants or ascendants; (b) An attorney cannot, without the consent of his client, be examined as to any communication made by the client to him, or his advice given thereon in the course of, or with a view to, professional employment, nor can an attorney's secretary, stenographer, or clerk be examined, without the consent of the client and his employer, concerning any fact the knowledge of which has been acquired in such capacity; (c) A person authorized to practice medicine, surgery or obstetrics cannot in a civil case, without the consent of the patient, be examined as to any advice or treatment given by him or any information which he may have acquired in attending such patient in a professional capacity, which information was necessary to enable him to act in that capacity, and which would blacken the reputation of the patient; (d) A minister or priest cannot, without the consent of the person making the confession, be examined as to any confession made to or any advice given by him in his professional character in the course of discipline enjoined by the church to which the minister or priest belongs; (e) A public officer cannot be examined during his term of office or afterwards, as to communications made to him in official confidence, when the court finds that the public interest would suffer by the disclosure. (*130 Rule 24*)

Testimonial privilege; admissions and confessions

No person may be compelled to testify against his parents, other direct ascendants, children or other direct descendants. (*130 Rule 25*). The act, declaration or omission of a party as to a relevant fact may be given in evidence against him. (*130 Rule 26*)

One type of act that can be given in evidence against the accused is flight. In criminal law, flight means an act of evading the course of justice by voluntarily withdrawing oneself to avoid arrest or detention or the institution or continuance of criminal proceedings. The unexplained flight of the accused person may, as a general rule, be taken as evidence having tendency to establish his guilt. In fact, we have held that once an accused escapes from prison or confinement or jumps bail or flees to a foreign country, he loses his standing in court, and unless he surrenders or submits himself to its jurisdiction, he is deemed to have waived any right to seek relief from the court. (*GR 134245, 1 Dec 00*)

In civil cases, an offer of compromise is not an admission of any liability, and is not admissible in evidence against the offeror. In criminal cases, except those involving quasi-offenses (criminal negligence) or those allowed by law to be compromised, an offer of compromise by the accused may be received in evidence as an implied admission of guilt. A plea of guilty later withdrawn, or an unaccepted offer of a plea of guilty to a lesser offense, is not admissible in evidence against the accused who made the plea or offer. An offer to pay or the payment of medical, hospital or other expenses occasioned by an injury is not admissible in evidence as proof of civil or criminal liability for the injury. (*130 Rule 27*)

A plea for forgiveness may be considered as analogous to an attempt to compromise. In criminal cases, except those involving quasi-offense (criminal negligence) or those allowed by law to be compromised, an offer of compromise by the accused may be received in evidence as an implied admission of guilt. No one would ask for forgiveness unless he had committed some wrong, for to forgive means to absolve, to pardon, to cease to feel resentment against on account of wrong committed; give up claim to requital from or retribution upon an offender . (*GR 117217, 2 Dec 96*)

The rights of a party cannot be prejudiced by an act, declaration, or omission of another, except as hereinafter provided. (*130 Rule 28*). The act or declaration of a partner or agent of the party within the scope of his authority and during the existence of the partnership or agency, may be given in evidence against such party after the partnership or agency is shown by evidence other than such act or declaration. The same rule applies to the act or declaration of a joint owner, joint debtor, or other person jointly interested with the party. (*130 Rule 29*). The act or declaration of a conspirator relating to the conspiracy and during its existence, may be given in evidence against the co-conspirator after the conspiracy is shown by evidence other than such act or declaration. (*130 Rule 30*).Where one derives title to property from another, the act, declaration, or omission of the latter, while holding the title, in relation to the property, is evidence against the former. (*130 Rule 31*). An act or declaration made in the presence and within the hearing or observation of a party who does or says nothing when the act or declaration is such as naturally to call for action or comment if not true, and when proper and possible for him to do so, may be given in evidence against him.(*130 Rule 32*).The declaration of an accused acknowledging his guilt of the offense charged, or of any offense necessarily included therein, may be given in evidence against him. (*130 Rule 33*)

The *res inter alios acta* rule provides that the rights of a party cannot be prejudiced by an act, declaration, or omission of another. Consequently, an extrajudicial confession is binding only upon the confessant and is not admissible against his co-accused. The reason for the rule is that, on a principle of good faith and mutual convenience, a man's own acts are binding upon himself, and are evidence against him. So are his conduct and declarations. Yet it would not only be rightly inconvenient, but also manifestly unjust, that a man should be bound by the acts of mere unauthorized strangers; and if a party ought not to be bound by the acts of strangers, neither ought their acts or conduct be used as evidence against him. (*GR 144621, 9 May 03*)

A confession constitutes evidence of high order since it is supported by the strong presumption that no person of normal mind would deliberately and knowingly confess to a crime unless prompted by truth and his conscience. This presumption of spontaneity and voluntariness stands unless the defense proves otherwise. (*GR 91694, 14 Mar 97*)

Previous conduct as evidence

Evidence that one did or did not do a certain thing at one time is not admissible to prove that he did or did not do the same or a similar thing at another time; but it may be received to prove a specific intent or knowledge, identity, plan, system, scheme, habit, custom or usage, and the like. (*130 Rule 34*)

An offer in writing to pay a particular sum of money or to deliver a written instrument or specific personal property is, if rejected without valid cause, equivalent to the actual production and tender of the money, instrument, or property. (*130 Rule 35*)

Testimonial knowledge; hearsay excluded

A witness can testify only to those facts which he knows of his personal knowledge; that is, which are derived from his own perception, except as otherwise provided. (*130 Rule 36*)

It is a hornbook doctrine of evidence that a witness can testify only to those facts which he knows of his personal knowledge, which means those facts which are derived from his perception. A witness may not testify as to what he merely learned from others either because he was told or read or heard the same. Such testimony is considered hearsay and may not be received as proof of the truth of what he has learned. The hearsay rule is based upon serious concerns about the trustworthiness and reliability of hearsay evidence inasmuch as such evidence are not given under oath or solemn affirmation and, more importantly, have not been subjected to cross-examination by opposing counsel to test the perception, memory, veracity, and articulateness of the out-of-court declarant or actor upon whose reliability on which the worth of the out-of-court statement depends. (*GR 151458, 31 Aug 06*)

The declaration of a dying person, made under the consciousness of an impending death, may be received in any case wherein his death is the subject of inquiry, as evidence of the cause and surrounding circumstances of such death. The declaration made by a person deceased, or unable to testify, against the interest of the declarant, if the fact asserted in the declaration was at the time it was made so far contrary to declarant's own interest, that a reasonable man in his position would not have made the declaration unless he believed it to be true, may be received in evidence against himself or his successors in interest and against third persons. The act or declaration of a person deceased, or unable to testify, in respect to the pedigree of another person related to him by birth or marriage, may be received in evidence where it occurred before the controversy, and the relationship between the two persons is shown by evidence other than such act or declaration. The word "pedigree" includes relationship, family genealogy, birth, marriage, death, the dates when and the places where these facts occurred, and the names of the relatives. It embraces also facts of family history intimately connected with pedigree. The reputation or tradition existing in a family previous to the controversy, in respect to the pedigree of any one of its members, may be received in evidence if the witness testifying thereon be also a member of the family, either by consanguinity or affinity. Entries in family bibles or other family books or charts, engraving on rings, family portraits and the like, may be received as evidence of pedigree. Common reputation existing previous to the controversy, respecting facts of public or general interest more than thirty years old, or respecting marriage or moral character, may be given in evidence, Monuments and inscriptions in public places may be received as evidence of common reputation.(*130 Rule 37-41*)

A dying declaration, as an exception to the general rule on the inadmissibility of hearsay evidence, is entitled to highest credence because no person who knows of his impending death would make a careless and false accusation. When a person is at the point of death, every motive for falsehood is silenced and the mind is induced by the most powerful consideration to speak the truth. Such a declaration, made *in extremis* when the party is at the point of death and the mind is induced by the most powerful consideration to speak the truth, occasioned by a situation so solemn and awful, is considered by the law as creating an obligation equal to that which is created by a positive oath administered in a court of justice. The idea, more succinctly expressed, is that "truth sits on the lips of dying men." (*GR 105004, 24 Jul 97*).

As an exception to the hearsay rule, the requisites for its admissibility are as follows: (1) the declaration was made by the deceased under the consciousness of his impending death; (2) the deceased was at the time competent as a witness; (3) the declaration concerns the cause and surrounding circumstances of the declarant's death; and (4) it is offered in a criminal case wherein the declarant's death is the subject of inquiry. (*Ibid.*)

Statements made by a person while a startling occurrence is taking place or immediately prior or subsequent thereto with respect to the circumstances thereof, may be given in evidence as part of the *res gestae*. So, also, statements accompanying an equivocal act material to the issue, and giving it a legal significance, may be received as part of the *res gestae*. (*130 Rule 42*)

Res gestae is a Latin phrase which literally means "things done." As an exception to the hearsay rule, it refers to those exclamations and statements by either the participants, victims, or spectators to a crime immediately before, during or immediately after the commission of the crime, when the circumstances are such that the statements were made as spontaneous reactions or utterances inspired by the excitement of the occasion, and there was no opportunity for the declarant to deliberate and fabricate a false statement. The reason for the rule is human experience. It has been shown that under certain external circumstances of physical or mental shock, the state of nervous excitement which occurs in a spectator may produce a spontaneous and sincere response to the actual sensations and perceptions produced by the external shock. As the statements or utterances are made under the immediate and uncontrolled domination of the senses, rather than reason and reflection, such statements or utterances may be taken as expressing the real belief of the speaker as to the facts he just observed. The spontaneity of the declaration is such that the declaration itself may be regarded as the event speaking through the declarant rather than the declarant speaking for himself. (*GR 146161, 17 Jul 06*)

For the admission of the *res gestae* in evidence, the following requisites must be met: (1) that the principal act or the *res gestae* be a startling occurrence; (2) the statement is spontaneous or was made before the declarant had time to contrive or devise, and the statement is made during the occurrence or immediately or subsequent thereto; and (3) the statement made must concern the occurrence in question and its immediately attending circumstances. (*Ibid.*)

Behavioral Response
There is no standard form of human behavioral response when one is confronted with a strange,

startling, or frightful experience. Witnessing a crime is an unusual experience that elicits different reactions from the witnesses, and for which no clear-cut standard form of behavior can be drawn. (*GR 120547, 29 Jan 01*)

The behavior or reaction of every person to a certain event cannot, however, be predicted with accuracy, and may be dealt with in any way by the victim whose testimony may be given full credence so long as her credibility is not tainted by any modicum of doubt. (*GR 140736-39, 04 Feb 03*)

It is a settled jurisprudence that different people react differently to a given situation and there is no standard form of behavioral response when one is confronted with a strange, startling or frightful experience. One person's spontaneous response may be aggression while another person's reaction may be cold indifference. (*GR 133739, 29 May 02*)

There is no standard form of behavioral response when one is confronted with a startling, strange or frightful experience. The initial reticence of witnesses to volunteer information about a criminal case and their aversion to be involved in criminal investigations due to fear of reprisal is not uncommon. (*GR 139879, 8 May 03*)

Thus: "Considering that appellant himself admitted that T.... had no participation in the murder, the fact that he fled the scene with appellant should not by itself be taken against him." (*Ibid.*)

Entries and records
Entries made at, or near the time of the transactions to which they refer, by a person

deceased, or unable to testify, who was in a position to know the facts therein stated, may be received as *prima facie* evidence, if such person made the entries in his professional capacity or in the performance of duty and in the ordinary or regular course of business or duty. Entries in official records made in the performance of his duty by a public officer of the Philippines, or by a person in the performance of a duty specially enjoined by law, are *prima facie* evidence of the facts therein stated. Evidence of statements of matters of interest to persons engaged in an occupation contained in a list, register, periodical, or other published compilations admissible as tending to prove the truth of any relevant matter so stated if that compilation is published for use by persons engaged in that occupation and is generally used and relied upon by them therein. A published treatise, periodical or pamphlet on a subject of history, law, science or art is admissible as tending to prove the truth of a matter stated therein if the court takes judicial notice, or a witness expert in the subject testifies, that the writer of the statement in the treatise, periodical or pamphlet is recognized in his profession or calling as expert in the subject. The testimony or deposition of a witness deceased or unable to testify, given in a former case or proceeding, judicial or administrative, involving the same parties and subject matter, may be given in evidence against the adverse party who had the opportunity to cross-examine him.(*130 Rule 43-47*)

It has been said that where, regardless of the truth or falsity of a statement, the fact that it has been made is relevant, the hearsay rule does not apply, and the statement may be shown. Evidence as to the making of such statement is not secondary but primary, for the statement itself may constitute a fact in issue, or be circumstantially relevant as to the existence of such a fact. (*GR 154087, 25 Oct 05*)

Opinion rule

The opinion of a witness is not admissible, except as indicated in the following. The opinion of a witness on a matter requiring special knowledge, skill, experience or training which he is shown to possess, may be received in evidence. The opinion of a witness for which proper basis is given, may be received in evidence regarding: (a) the identity of a person about whom he has adequate knowledge; (b) a handwriting with which he has sufficient familiarity; and (c) the mental sanity of a person with whom he is sufficiently acquainted. The witness may also testify on his impressions of the motion, behavior, condition or appearance of a person. (130 Rule 48-50)

Suffice it to state, expert opinion evidence is to be considered or weighed by the court like any other testimony, in the light of their own general knowledge and experience upon the subject of inquiry. The probative force of the testimony of an expert does not lie in a mere statement of the theory or opinion of the expert, but rather in the aid that he can render to the courts in showing the facts which serve as a basis for his criterion and the reasons upon which the logic of his conclusion is founded. (*GR 145002, 24 Jan 06*)

In addition, the inclusion or exclusion by the expert of factors or elements that should or should not be considered in the determination of his opinion is to be considered in determining the weight to be attached to his testimony. (Ibid.)

Thus--

Expert testimony no doubt constitutes evidence worthy of meriting consideration, although not exclusive on questions of professional character. The courts of justice, however, are not bound to submit their findings necessarily to such testimony; they are free to weigh them, and they can give or refuse to give them any value as proof, or they can even counterbalance such evidence with other elements of conviction which may have been adduced during the trial. (*Ibid.*)

Handwriting experts are usually helpful in the examination of forged documents because of the technical procedure involved in analyzing them. But resort to these experts is not mandatory or indispensable to the examination or the comparison of handwriting. A finding of forgery does not depend entirely on the testimonies of handwriting experts, because the judge must conduct an independent examination of the questioned signature in order to arrive at a reasonable conclusion as to its authenticity. (*GR 140472, 10 Jun 02*)

Character evidence

In Criminal Cases, the accused may prove his good moral character which is pertinent to the moral trait involved in the offense charged. Unless in rebuttal, the prosecution may not prove his bad moral character which is pertinent to the moral trait involved in the offense charged. The good or bad moral character of the offended party may be proved if it tends to establish in any reasonable degree the probability or improbability of the offense charged. In Civil Cases, evidence of the moral character of a party in a civil case is admissible only when pertinent to the issue of character involved in the case. (*130 Rule 51*)

Character is defined to be the possession by a person of certain qualities of mind and morals, distinguishing him from others. It is the opinion generally entertained of a person derived from the common report of the people who are acquainted with him; his reputation. "Good moral character" includes all the elements essential to make up such a character; among these are common honesty and veracity, especially in all professional intercourse; a character that measures up as good among people of the community in which the person lives, or that is up to the standard of the average citizen; that status which attaches to a man of good behavior and upright conduct. (*GR 139070, 29 May 02*)

Chapter 10
Burden of proof; Presumptions

Burden of proof is the duty of a party to present evidence on the facts in issue necessary to establish his claim or defense by the amount of evidence required by law. (*131 Rule 1*)

The party, whether plaintiff or defendant, who asserts the affirmative of the issue has the burden of proof to obtain a favorable judgment. For the plaintiff, the burden of proof never parts. For the defendant, an affirmative defense is one which is not a denial of an essential ingredient in the plaintiff's cause of action, but one which, if established, will be a good defense – i.e. an "avoidance" of the claim. (*GR 147039, 27 Jan 06*)

In civil cases, the burden of proof may be on either the plaintiff or the defendant. It is on the latter, if in his answer he alleges an affirmative defense, which is not a denial of an essential ingredient in the plaintiff's cause of action, but is one which, if established, will be a good defense – i.e., an "avoidance" of the claim, which prima facie, the plaintiff already has because of the defendant's own admissions in the pleadings. (*GR 132604, 6 Mar 02*)

Conclusive presumptions

The following are instances of conclusive presumptions: (a) Whenever a party has, by his own declaration, act, or omission, intentionally and deliberately led another to believe a particular thing true, and to act upon such belief, he cannot, in any litigation arising out of such declaration, act or omission, be permitted to falsify it: (b) The tenant is not permitted to deny the title of his landlord at the time of the commencement of the relation of landlord and tenant between them. (*131 Rule 2*)

Conclusive presumptions have been defined as "inferences which the law makes so peremptory that it will not allow them to be overturned by any contrary proof however strong." (*GR 144268, 30 Aug 06*)

Disputable presumptions

The following presumptions are satisfactory if uncontradicted, but may be contradicted and overcome by other evidence:

(a) That a person is innocent of crime or wrong;

(b) That an unlawful act was done with an unlawful intent;

(c) That a person intends the ordinary consequences of his voluntary act;

(d) That a person take ordinary care of his concerns;

(e) That evidence willfully suppressed would be adverse if produced;

(f) That money paid by one to another was due to the latter;

(g) That a thing delivered by one to another belonged to the latter;

(h) That an obligation delivered up to the debtor has been paid;

(i) That prior rents or installments had been paid when a receipt for the later ones is produced;

(j) That a person found in possession of a thing taken in the doing of a recent wrongful act is the taker and the doer of the whole act; otherwise, that things which a person possesses, or exercises acts of ownership over, are owned by him;

(k) That a person in possession of an order on himself for the payment of the money, or the delivery of anything, has paid the money or delivered the thing accordingly;

(l) That a person acting in a public office was regularly appointed or elected to it;

(m) That official duty has been regularly performed;

(n) That a court, or judge acting as such, whether in the Philippines or elsewhere, was acting in the lawful exercise of jurisdiction;

(o) That all the matters within an issue raised in a case were laid before the court and passed upon by it; and in like manner that all matters within an issue raised in a dispute submitted for arbitration were laid before the arbitrators and passed upon by them;

(p) That private transactions have been fair and regular;

(q) That the ordinary course of business has been followed;

(r) That there was a sufficient consideration for a contract;

(s) That a negotiable instrument was given or indorsed for a sufficient consideration;

(t) That an indorsement of a negotiable instrument was made before the instrument was overdue and at the place where the instrument is dated;

(u) That a writing is truly dated;

(v) That a letter duly directed and mailed was received in the regular course of the mail;

(w) That after an absence of seven years, it being unknown whether or not the absentee still lives, he is considered dead for all purposes, except for those of succession.

The absentee shall not be considered dead for the purpose of opening his succession till after an absence of ten years. If he disappeared after the age of seventy-five years, an absence of five years shall be sufficient in order that his succession may be opened.

The following shall be considered dead for all purposes including the division of the estate among the heirs:

(1) A person on board a vessel lost during a sea voyage, or an aircraft which is missing, who has not been heard of for four years since the loss of the vessel or aircraft;

(2) A member of the armed forces who has taken part in armed hostilities, and has been missing for four years;

(3) A person who has been in danger of death under other circumstances and whose existence has not been known for four years;

(4) If a married person has been absent for four consecutive years, the spouse present may contract a subsequent marriage if he or she has a well-founded belief that the absent spouse is already dead. In case of disappearance, where there is danger of death under the circumstances hereinabove provided an absence of only two years shall be sufficient for the purpose of contracting a subsequent marriage. However, in any case, before marrying again, the spouse present must institute a summary proceeding as provided in the Family Code and in the rules for a declaration of presumptive death of the absentee, without prejudice to the effect of reappearance of the absent spouse.

(x) That acquiescence resulted from a belief that the thing acquiesced in was conformable to the law or fact;

(y) That things have happened according to the ordinary course of nature and the ordinary habits of life;

(z) That persons acting as copartners have entered into a contract of co-partnership;

(aa) That a man and woman deporting themselves as husband and wife have entered into a lawful contract of marriage;

(bb) That property acquired by a man and woman who are capacitated to marry each other and who live exclusively with each other as husband and wife without the benefit of marriage or under a void marriage, has been obtained by their joint efforts, work or industry.

(cc) That in cases of cohabitation by a man and a woman who are not capacitated to marry each other and who have acquired property through their actual joint contribution of money, property or industry, such contributions and their corresponding shares including joint deposits of money and evidences of credit are equal.

(dd) That if the marriage is terminated and the mother contracted another marriage within three hundred days after such termination of the former marriage, these rules shall govern in the absence of proof to the contrary:

(1) A child born before one hundred eighty days after the solemnization of the subsequent marriage is considered to have been conceived during the former marriage, provided it be born within three hundred days after the termination of the former marriage;

(2) A child born after one hundred eighty days following the celebration of the subsequent marriage

is considered to have been conceived during such marriage, even though it be born within the three hundred days after the termination of the former marriage.

(ee) That a thing once proved to exist continues as long as is usual with things of that nature;

(ff) That the law has been obeyed;

(gg) That a printed or published book, purporting to be printed or published by public authority, was so printed or published;

(hh) That a printed or published book, purporting to contain reports of cases adjudged in tribunals of the country where the book is published, contains correct reports of such cases;

(ii) That a trustee or other person whose duty it was to convey real property to a particular person has actually conveyed it to him when such presumption is necessary to perfect the title of such person or his successor in interest;

(jj) That except for purposes of succession, when two persons perish in the same calamity, such as wreck, battle, or conflagration, and it is not shown who died first, and there are no particular circumstances from which it can be inferred, the survivorship is determined from the probabilities resulting from the strength and age of the sexes, according to the following rules:

1. If both were under the age of fifteen years, the older is deemed to have survived;

2. If both were above the age of sixty, the younger is deemed to have survived;

3. If one is under fifteen and the other above sixty, the former is deemed to have survived;

4. If both be over fifteen and under sixty, and the sex be different, the male is deemed to have survived; if the sex be the same, the older;

5. If one be under fifteen or over sixty, and the other between those ages, the latter is deemed to have survived.

(kk) That if there is a doubt, as between two or more persons who are called to succeed each other, as to which of them died first, whoever alleges the death of one prior to the other, shall prove the same; in the absence of proof, they shall be considered to have died at the same time. (*131 Rule 3*)

There is no presumption of legitimacy or illegitimacy of a child born after three hundred days following the dissolution of the marriage or the separation of the spouses. Whoever alleges the legitimacy or illegitimacy of such child must prove his allegation. (*131 Rule 4*)

Chapter 11
Examination of Witnesses

The examination of witnesses presented in a trial or hearing shall be done in open court, and under oath or affirmation. Unless the witness is incapacitated to speak, or the question calls for a different mode of answer, the answers of the witness shall be given orally. (*132 Rule 1*). The entire proceedings of a trial or hearing, including the questions propounded to a witness and his answers thereto, the statements made by the judge or any of the parties, counsel, or witnesses with reference to the case, shall be recorded by means of shorthand or stenotype or by other means of recording found suitable by the court. A transcript of the record of the proceedings made by the official stenographer, stenotypist or recorder and certified as correct by him shall be deemed *prima facie* a correct statement of such proceedings. (*132 Rule 2*)

A witness must answer questions, although his answer may tend to establish a claim against him. However, it is the right of a witness: (1) To be protected from irrelevant, improper, or insulting questions, and from harsh or insulting demeanor; (2) Not to be detained longer than the interests of justice require; (3) Not to be examined except only as to matters pertinent to the issue; (4) Not to give an answer which will tend to subject him to a penalty for an offense unless otherwise provided by law; or (5) Not to give an answer which will tend to degrade his reputation, unless it be to the very fact at issue or to a fact from which the fact in issue would be presumed. But a witness must answer to the fact of his previous final conviction for an offense. (*132 Rule 3*)

The order in which an individual witness may be examined is as follows: (a) Direct examination by the proponent; (b) Cross-examination by the opponent; (c) Re-direct examination by the proponent; (d) Re-cross-examination by the opponent. (*132 Rule 4*)

Direct examination is the examination-in-chief of a witness by the party presenting him on the facts relevant to the issue. (*132 Rule 5*). Upon the termination of the direct examination, the witness may be cross-examined by the adverse party as to any matters stated in the direct examination, or connected therewith, with sufficient fullness and freedom to test his accuracy and truthfulness and freedom from interest or bias, or the reverse, and to elicit all important facts bearing upon the issue. (*132 Rule 6*). After the cross-examination of the witness has been concluded, he may be re-examined by the party calling him, to explain or supplement his answers given during the cross-examination. On re-direct examination, questions on matters not dealt with during the cross-examination, may be allowed by the court in its discretion. (*132 Rule 7*). Upon the conclusion of the re-direct examination, the adverse party may re-cross-examine the witness on matters stated in his re-direct examination, and also on such other matters as may be allowed by the court in its discretion. (*132 Rule 8*)

After the examination of a witness by both sides has been concluded, the witness cannot be recalled without leave of the court. The court will grant or withhold leave in its discretion, as the interests of justice may require. (*132 Rule 9*)

The cross-examination of a witness is a prerogative of the party against whom the witness is called. The purpose of cross-examination is to test the truth or accuracy of the statements of a witness made on direct examination. The party against whom the witness testifies may deem any further examination unnecessary and instead rely on any other evidence theretofore adduced or thereafter to be adduced or on what would be believed is the perception of the court thereon. Certainly, the trial court is not bound to give full weight to the testimony of a witness on direct examination merely because he is not cross-examined by the other party. (*GR 146697, 23 Jul 05*)

Leading and misleading questions

A question which suggests to the witness the answer which the examining party desires is a leading question. It is not allowed, except: (a) On cross examination; (b) On preliminary matters; (c) When there is difficulty in getting direct and intelligible answers from a witness who is ignorant, or a child of tender years, or is of feeble mind, or a deaf-mute; (d) Of an unwilling or hostile witness; or (e) Of a witness who is an adverse party or an officer, director, or managing agent of a public or private corporation or of a partnership or association which is an adverse party. A misleading question is one which assumes as true a fact not yet testified to by the witness, or contrary to that which he has previously stated. It is not allowed. (*132 Rule 10*)

As a rule, leading questions are not allowed. However, the rules provide for exceptions when the witness is a child of tender years as it is usually difficult for such child to state facts without prompting or suggestion. Leading questions are necessary to coax the truth out of their reluctant lips. (*GR 142556, 5 Feb 03*)

Impeachment of a witness

A witness may be impeached by the party against whom he was called, by contradictory evidence, by evidence that his general reputation for truth, honesty, or integrity is bad, or by evidence that he has made at other times statements inconsistent with his present testimony, but not by evidence of particular wrongful acts, except that it may be shown by the examination of the witness, or the record of the judgment, that he has been convicted of an offense. A party may not impeach his own witness. A witness may be considered as unwilling or hostile only if so declared by the court upon adequate showing of his adverse interest, unjustified reluctance to testify, or his having misled the party into calling him to the witness stand. The unwilling or hostile witness so declared, or the witness who is an adverse party, may be impeached by the party presenting him in all respects as if he had been called by the adverse party, except by evidence of his bad character. He may also be impeached and cross-examined by the adverse party, but such cross-examination must only be on the subject matter of his examination-in-chief. Before a witness can be impeached by evidence that he has made at other times statements inconsistent with his present testimony, the statements must be related to him, with the circumstances of the times and places and the persons present, and he must be asked whether he made such statements, and if so, allowed to explain them. If the statements be in writing they must be shown to the witness before any question is put to him concerning them. (*132 Rule 11-13*).

A person who produces a witness vouches for him as being worthy of credit, and that a direct attack upon the veracity of the witness "would enable the party to destroy the witness, if he spoke against him, and to make him a good witness, if he spoke for him, with the means in his hands of destroying his credit, if he spoke against him." (*GR 156284, 6 Feb 07*)

Evidence of the good character of a witness is not admissible until such character has been impeached. (*132 Rule 14*)

On any trial or hearing, the judge may exclude from the court any witness not at the time under examination, so that he may not hear the testimony of other witnesses. The judge may also cause witnesses to be kept separate and to be prevented from conversing with one another until all shall have been examined. (*132 Rule 15*)

A witness may be allowed to refresh his memory respecting a fact, by anything written or recorded by himself or under his direction at the time when the fact occurred, or immediately thereafter, or at any other time when the fact was fresh in his memory and he knew that the same was correctly written or recorded; but in such case the writing or record must be produced and may be inspected by the adverse party, who may, if he chooses, cross-examine the witness upon it, and may read it in evidence. So, also, a witness may testify from such a writing or record, though he retain no recollection of the particular facts, if he is able to swear that the writing or record correctly stated the transaction when made; but such evidence must be received with caution. When part of an act, declaration, conversation, writing or record is given in evidence by one party, the whole of the same subject may be inquired into by the other, and when a detached act, declaration, conversation, writing or record is given in evidence, any other act, declaration, conversation, writing or record necessary to its understanding may also be given in evidence. Whenever a writing is shown to a witness, it may be inspected by the adverse party. (*132 Rule 16-18*)

Chapter 12
Documents; Authentication and Proof

For the purpose of their presentation in evidence, documents are either public or private. Public documents are: (a) the written official acts, or records of the official acts of the sovereign authority, official bodies and tribunals, and public officers, whether of the Philippines, or of a foreign country; (b) documents acknowledged before a notary public except last wills and testaments; and (c) Public records, kept in the Philippines, of private documents required by law to be entered therein. All other writings are private. (*132 Rule 19*)

A notarized document carries the evidentiary weight conferred upon it with respect to its due execution, and it has in its favor the presumption of regularity which may only be rebutted by evidence so clear, strong and convincing as to exclude all controversy as to the falsity of the certificate. Absent such, the presumption must be upheld. The burden of proof to overcome the presumption of due execution of a notarial document lies on the one contesting the same. (*GR 125283, 10 Feb 06*)

Before any private document offered as authentic is received in evidence, its due execution and authenticity must be proved either: (a) by anyone who saw the document executed or written; or (b) by evidence of the genuineness of the signature or handwriting of the maker. Any other private document need only be identified as that which it is claimed to be. (*132 Rule 20*)

Where a private document is more than thirty years old, is produced from a custody in which it would naturally be found if genuine, and is unblemished by any alterations or circumstances of suspicion, no other evidence of its authenticity need be given.(*132 Rule 21*)

The handwriting of a person may be proved by any witness who believes it to be the handwriting of such person because he has seen the person write, or has seen writing purporting to be his upon which the witness has acted or been charged, and has thus acquired knowledge of the handwriting of such person. Evidence respecting the handwriting may also be given by a comparison, made by the witness or the court, with writings admitted or treated as genuine by the party against whom the evidence is offered, or proved to be genuine to the satisfaction of the judge. (*132 Rule 22*)

Documents consisting of entries in public records made in the performance of a duty by a public officer are *prima facie* evidence of the facts therein stated. All other public documents are evidence, even against a third person, of the fact which gave rise to their execution and of the date of the latter. (*132 Rule 23*)

The record of public documents referred, when admissible for any purpose, may be evidenced by an official publication thereof or by a copy attested by the officer having the legal custody of the record, or by his deputy, and accompanied, if the record is not kept in the Philippines, with a certificate that such officer has the custody. If the office in which the record is kept is in a foreign country, the certificate may be made by a secretary of the embassy or legation, consul general, consul, vice consul, or consular agent or by any officer in the foreign service of the Philippines stationed in the foreign country in which the record is kept, and authenticated by the seal of his office. (*132 Rule 24*)

Whenever a copy of a document or record is attested for the purpose of evidence, the attestation must state, in substance, that the copy is a correct copy of the original, or a specific part thereof, as the case may be. The attestation must be under the official seal of the attesting officer, if there be any, or if he be the clerk of a court having a seal, under the seal of such court. (*132 Rule 25*)

Any public record, an official copy of which is admissible in evidence, must not be removed from the office in which it is kept, except upon order of a court where the inspection of the record is essential to the just determination of a pending case. An authorized public record of a private document may be proved by the original record, or by a copy thereof, attested by the legal custodian of the record, with an appropriate certificate that such officer has the custody. A written statement signed by an officer having the custody of an official record or by his deputy that after diligent search no record or entry of a specified tenor is found to exist in the records of his office, accompanied by a certificate as above provided, is admissible as evidence that the records of his office contain no such record or entry. (*132 Rule 26-28*)

Judicial record and notarial documents

Any judicial record may be impeached by evidence of: (a) want of jurisdiction in the court or judicial officer, (b) collusion between the parties, or (c) fraud in the party offering the record, in respect to the proceedings. Every instrument duly acknowledged or proved and certified as provided by law, may be presented in evidence without further proof, the certificate of acknowledgment being *prima facie* evidence of the execution of the instrument or document involved.(*132 Rule 29-30*)

The party producing a document as genuine which has been altered and appears to have been altered after its execution, in a part material to the question in dispute, must account for the alteration. He may show that the alteration was made by another, without his concurrence, or was made with the consent of the parties affected by it, or was otherwise properly or innocently made, or that the alteration did not change the meaning or language of the instrument. If he fails to do that, the document shall not be admissible in evidence. There shall be no difference between sealed and unsealed private documents insofar as their admissibility as evidence is concerned. (*132 Rule 31-32*)

Chapter 13
Offer and Objection

The court shall consider no evidence which has not been formally offered. The purpose for which the evidence is offered must be specified. As regards the testimony of a witness, the offer must be made at the time the witness is called to testify. Documentary and object evidence shall be offered after the presentation of a party's testimonial evidence. Such offer shall be done orally unless allowed by the court to be done in writing, (*132 Rule 34-35*)

The trial court is bound to consider only the testimonial evidence presented and exclude the documents not offered. Documents which may have been identified and marked as exhibits during pre-trial or trial but which were not formally offered in evidence cannot in any manner be treated as evidence. Neither can such unrecognized proof be assigned any evidentiary weight and value. It must be stressed that there is a significant distinction between identification of documentary evidence and its formal offer. The former is done in the course of the pre-trial, and trial is accompanied by the marking of the evidence as an exhibit; while the latter is done only when the party rests its case. The mere fact that a particular document is identified and marked as an exhibit does not mean that it has already been offered as part of the evidence. It must be emphasized that any evidence which a party desires to submit for the consideration of the court must formally be offered by the party; otherwise, it is excluded and rejected. (*GR 155483, 27 Apr 07*)

Thus—

No evidence shall be allowed to be presented and offered during the trial in support of a party's evidence-in-chief other than those that had been identified below and pre-marked during the pre-trial. Any other evidence not indicated or listed below shall be considered waived by the parties. However, the Court, in its discretion, may allow introduction of additional evidence in the following cases: (a) those to be used on cross-examination or re-cross-examination for impeachment purposes; (b) those presented on re-direct examination to explain or supplement the answers of a witness during the cross-examination; (c) those to be utilized for rebuttal or sur-rebuttal purposes; and (d) those not available during the pre-trial proceedings despite due diligence on the part of the party offering the same.

It is apparent from the foregoing provision that both parties should obtain, gather, collate, and list all their respective pieces of evidence— whether testimonial, documentary, or object—even prior to the preliminary conference before the clerk of court or at the latest before the scheduled pre-trial conference. Otherwise, pieces of evidence not identified or marked during the pre-trial proceedings are deemed waived and rendered inutile. The parties should strictly adhere to the principle of "laying one's cards on the table." In the light of these issuances and in order to obviate interminable delay in case processing, the parties and lawyers should closely conform to the requirement that the offer of evidence must be done orally on the day scheduled for the presentation of the last witness. (*Ibid.*)

Objection to evidence offered orally must be made immediately after the offer is made. Objection to a question propounded in the course of the oral examination of a witness shall be made as soon as the grounds therefor shall become reasonably apparent. An offer of evidence in writing shall be objected to within three (3) days after notice of the offer unless a different period is allowed by the court. In any case, the grounds for the objections must be specified. (*132 Rule 36*)

When it becomes reasonably apparent in the course of the examination of a witness that the questions being propounded are of the same class as those to which objection has been made, whether such objection was sustained or overruled, it shall not be necessary to repeat the objection, it being sufficient for the adverse party to record his continuing objection to such class of questions. (*132 Rule 37*)

The ruling of the court must be given immediately after the objection is made, unless the court desires to take a reasonable time to inform itself on the question presented; but the ruling shall always be made during the trial and at such time as will give the party against whom it is made an opportunity to meet the situation presented by the ruling. The reason for sustaining or overruling an objection need not be stated. However, if the objection is based on two or more grounds, a ruling sustaining the objection on one or some of them must specify the ground or grounds relied upon. (*132 Rule 38*). Should a witness answer the question before the adverse party had the opportunity to voice fully its objection to the same, and such objection is found to be meritorious, the court shall sustain the objection and order the answer given to be stricken off the record. On proper motion, the court may also order the striking out of answers which are incompetent, irrelevant, or otherwise improper. (*132 Rule 39*)

If documents or things offered in evidence are excluded by the court, the offeror may have the same attached to or made part of the record. If the evidence excluded is oral, the offeror may state for the record the same and other personal circumstances of the witness and the substance of the proposed testimony. (*132 Rule 40*)

Chapter 14
Quantum of Proof

In civil cases, the party having the burden of proof must establish his case by a preponderance of evidence. In determining where the preponderance or superior weight of evidence on the issues involved lies, the court may consider all the facts and circumstances of the case, the witnesses' manner of testifying, their intelligence, their means and opportunity of knowing the facts to which they are testifying, the nature of the facts to which they testify, the probability or improbability of their testimony, their interest or want of interest, and also their personal credibility so far as the same may legitimately appear upon the trial. The court may also consider the number of witnesses, though the preponderance is not necessarily with the greater number. (*133 Rule 1*)

In civil cases, basic is the rule that the party making allegations has the burden of proving them by a preponderance of evidence. Moreover, parties must rely on the strength of their own evidence, not upon the weakness of the defense offered by their opponent. This principle holds true, especially when the latter has had no opportunity to present evidence because of a default order. Needless to say, the extent of the relief that may be granted can only be as much as has been alleged and proved with preponderant evidence required. (*GR 151098, 21 Mar 06*)

When a defendant fails to file an answer, the court shall proceed to render judgment granting the claimant such relief as his pleading may warrant, subject to the court's discretion on whether to require the presentation of evidence ex parte. The same provision also sets down guidelines on the nature and extent of the relief that may be granted. In particular, the court's judgment shall not exceed the amount or be different in kind from that prayed. (*Ibid.*)

In a criminal case, the accused is entitled to an acquittal, unless his guilt is shown beyond reasonable doubt. Proof beyond reasonable doubt does not mean such a degree of proof as, excluding possibility of error, produces absolute certainty. Moral certainty only is required, or that degree of proof which produces conviction in an unprejudiced mind. An extrajudicial confession made by an accused, shall not be sufficient ground for conviction, unless corroborated by evidence *of corpus delicti. (133 Rule 2-3)*

It is basic and elemental that in criminal prosecutions, before the accused may be convicted of a crime, his guilt must be proven beyond reasonable doubt. Although the findings of fact made by trial courts are generally not disturbed on appeal, if there are substantial facts which were overlooked but which may alter the results of the case in favor of the accused, such facts should be taken into account by the appellate court. And where it appears that the trial court erred in the appreciation of the evidence on record or the lack of it, the factual findings of the trial court may be reversed. (*GR 166488, 31May 01*)

The Constitution mandates that an accused shall be presumed innocent until the contrary is proven beyond reasonable doubt. The prosecution has the burden to overcome such presumption of innocence by presenting the quantum of evidence required. Corollarily, the prosecution must rest on its own merits and must not rely on the weakness of the defense. If the prosecution fails to meet the required quantum of evidence, the defense may logically not even present evidence on its own behalf. In which case, the presumption of innocence shall prevail and hence, the accused shall be acquitted. However, once the presumption of innocence is overcome, the defense bears the burden of evidence to show reasonable doubt as to the guilt of the accused. Reasonable doubt is that doubt engendered by an investigation of the whole proof and an inability after such investigation to let the mind rest each upon the certainty of guilt. Absolute certainty of guilt is not demanded by the law to convict a criminal charge, but moral certainty is required as to every proposition of proof requisite to constitute the offense. (*GR 175593, 17 Oct 07*)

Identification evidence

The correct identification of the author of a crime should be the primal concern of criminal prosecution in any civilized legal system. Corollary to this is the actuality of the commission of the offense with the participation of the accused. All these must be proved by the State beyond reasonable doubt on the strength of its evidence and without solace from the weakness of the defense. Thus, even if the defense of the accused may be weak, the same is inconsequential if, in the first place, the prosecution failed to discharge the onus on his identity and culpability. The presumption of innocence dictates that it is for the people to demonstrate guilt and not for the accused to establish innocence. (*GR 134974, 8 Dec 00*)

The procedure for out-of-court identification and the test to determine the admissibility of such identification thus:

"x x x. Out-of-court identification is conducted by the police in various ways. It is done thru *show-ups* where the suspect alone is brought face to face with the witness for identification. It is done thru *mug shots* where photographs are shown to the witness to identify the suspect. It is also done thru *line-ups* where a witness identifies the suspect from a group of persons lined up for the purpose. Since corruption of *out-of-court* identification contaminates the integrity of *in-court* identification during the trial of the case, courts have fashioned out rules to assure its fairness and its compliance with the requirements of constitutional due process. In resolving the admissibility of and relying on out-of-court identification of suspects, courts have adopted the *totality of circumstances test* where they consider the following factors, *viz*: (1) the witness's opportunity to view the criminal at the time of the crime; (2) the witness' degree of attention at that time; (3) the accuracy of any prior description given by the witness; (4) the level of certainty demonstrated by the witness at the identification; (5) the length of time between the crime and the identification; and (6) the suggestiveness of the identification procedure." (*Ibid.*)

While eyewitness identification is significant, it is not as accurate and authoritative as the scientific forms of identification evidence such as the fingerprint or the DNA test result. Some authors even describe eyewitness evidence as 'inherently suspect.' Known causes of misidentification have been identified as follows:

"Identification testimony has at least three components. First, witnessing a crime, whether as a victim or a bystander, involves perception of an event actually occurring. Second, the witness must memorize details of the event. Third, the witness must be able to recall and communicate accurately. *Dangers of unreliability in eyewitness testimony arise at each of these three stages, for whenever people attempt to acquire, retain, and retrieve information accurately, they are limited by normal human fallibilities and suggestive influences.*" (*GR 141438-40, 03 Feb 03*)

Circumstantial evidence

Circumstantial evidence is sufficient for conviction if: (a) There is more than one circumstance; (b) The facts from which the inferences are derived are proven; and (c) The combination of all the circumstances is such as to produce a conviction beyond reasonable doubt. (*133 Rule 4*)

Direct evidence of the crime is not the only matrix wherefrom a trial court may draw its conclusion and finding of guilt. The rules of evidence allow a trial court to rely on circumstantial evidence to support its conclusion of guilt. Circumstantial evidence is that evidence which proves a fact or series of facts from which the facts in issue may be established by inference. At times, resort to circumstantial evidence is imperative since to insist on direct testimony would, in many cases, result in setting felons free and deny proper protection to the community. (*GR 164266, 23Jul 08*)

All the circumstances must be consistent with one another, consistent with the hypothesis that the accused is guilty, and at the same time inconsistent with the hypothesis that he is innocent. Thus, conviction based on circumstantial evidence can be upheld, provided that the circumstances proven constitute an unbroken chain which leads to one fair and reasonable conclusion that points to the accused, to the exclusion of all others, as the guilty person. (*Ibid.*)

The standard that should be observed by the courts in appreciating circumstantial evidence (as discussed in *GR 165884, 23 Apr 07*) is thus:

No general rule can be laid down as to the quantity of circumstantial evidence which in any case will suffice. All the circumstances proved must be consistent with each other, consistent with the hypothesis that the accused is guilty, and at the same time inconsistent with the hypothesis that he is innocent, and with every other rational hypothesis except that of guilt.

It has been said, and we believe correctly, that the circumstances proved should constitute an unbroken chain which leads to one fair and reasonable conclusion which points to the accused, to the exclusion of all others, as the guilty person. From all the circumstances, there should be a combination of evidence which in the ordinary and natural course of things, leaves no room for reasonable doubt as to his guilt. Stated in another way, where the inculpatory facts and circumstances are capable of two or more explanations, one of which is consistent with innocence and the other with guilt, the evidence does not fulfill the test of moral certainty and is not sufficient to convict the accused.

Substantial evidence

In cases filed before administrative or quasi-judicial bodies, a fact may be deemed established if it is supported by substantial evidence, or that amount of relevant evidence which a reasonable mind might accept as adequate to justify a conclusion. (*133 Rule 5*)

In administrative proceedings, the complainant has the burden of proving with substantial evidence the allegations in the complaint. While rules of evidence prevailing in courts of law and equity shall not be controlling, this assurance of a desirable flexibility in administrative procedure does not go as far as to justify orders without basis in evidence having rational probative force. (*GR 154108, 10 Dec 08*)

A finding of guilt in an administrative case would have to be sustained for as long as it is supported by substantial evidence that respondent has committed the acts stated in the complaint or formal charge. Substantial evidence has been defined as such relevant evidence as a reasonable mind might accept as adequate to support a conclusion. This is different from the degree of proof required in criminal proceedings, which calls for a finding of guilt beyond reasonable doubt. (*GR 172580, 23 Jul 08*)

Chapter 15
Other Points in Evidence Presentation

The court may stop the introduction of further testimony upon any particular point when the evidence upon it is already so full that more witnesses to the same point cannot be reasonably expected to be additionally persuasive. But this power should be exercised with caution. (*133 Rule 6*)

When a motion is based on facts not appearing of record the court may hear the matter on affidavits or depositions presented by the respective parties, but the court may direct that the matter be heard wholly or partly on oral testimony or depositions. (*133 Rule 7*)

A formal trial-type hearing is not at all times and in all instances essential to due process. It is enough that the parties are given a fair and reasonable opportunity to explain their respective sides of the controversy and to present evidence on which a fair decision can be based. (*GR 129958, 25 Nov 99*)

A "deposition," in its technical and appropriate sense, is the written testimony of a witness given in the course of a judicial proceeding, in advance of the trial or hearing upon oral examination or in response to written interrogatories and where an opportunity is given for cross-examination. A deposition may be taken at any time after the institution of any action, whenever necessary or convenient. (*GR 112710, 30 May 01*)

As likewise stated in GR 112710:

Under the original Rule 26 (a) of the Federal Rules of Civil Procedure, any party desiring to take depositions before answer was served was required to obtain leave of court. While the Rule did not indicate in what situations the court should grant such leave, the applicable principles are found in jurisprudence.

The general rule is that a plaintiff may not be permitted to take depositions before answer is served. Plaintiff must await joinder of issues because if the discovery is to deal with matters relevant to the case, it is difficult to know exactly what is relevant until some progress has been made toward developing the issues. Ordinarily, the issues are made up before the need for discovery arises, hence, prior to the time of delineation of the issues, the matter is in the control of the court.

There are instances, however, when a deposition is allowed to be taken before service of answer once jurisdiction has been acquired over the person or thing. Leave of court may be granted only in "exceptional" or "unusual" cases, and the decision is entirely within the discretion of the court. It should be granted only under "special circumstances" where conditions point to the necessity of presenting a strong case for allowance of the motion. There must be some "necessity" or "good reason" for taking the testimony immediately or that it would be prejudicial to the party seeking the order to be compelled to await joinder of issue. If the witness is aged or infirm, or about to leave the court's jurisdiction, or is only temporarily in the jurisdiction, leave may be granted. A general examination by deposition before answer however is premature and ordinarily not allowed, neither is mere avoidance of delay a sufficient reason.

While depositions may be used as evidence in court proceedings, they are generally not meant to be a substitute for the actual testimony in open court of a party or witness. Stated a bit differently, a deposition is not to be used when the deponent is at hand. Indeed, any deposition offered during a trial to prove the facts therein set out, in lieu of the actual oral testimony of the deponent in open court, may be opposed and excluded on the ground of hearsay. However, depositions may be used without the deponent being called to the witness stand by the proponent, provided the existence of certain

164

conditions is first satisfactorily established. (*GR 133154, 9 Dec 05*)

As a rule, the inadmissibility of testimony taken by deposition is anchored on the ground that such testimony is hearsay, *i.e.*, the party against whom it is offered has no opportunity to cross-examine the deponent at the time his testimony is offered. But as jurisprudence teaches, it matters not that opportunity for cross-examination was afforded during the taking of the deposition; for normally, the opportunity for cross-examination must be accorded a party at the time the testimonial evidence is actually presented against him during the trial or hearing. In fine, the act of cross-examining the deponent during the taking of the deposition cannot, without more, be considered a waiver of the right to object to its admissibility as evidence in the trial proper. (*Ibid.*)

While errors and irregularities in depositions as to notice, qualifications of the officer conducting the deposition, and manner of taking the deposition are deemed waived if not objected to before or during the taking of the deposition, objections to the competency of a witness or the competency, relevancy, or materiality of testimony may be made for the first time at the trial and need not be made at the time of the taking of the deposition, unless they could be obviated at that point. (*Ibid.*)

Deposition is chiefly a mode of discovery, the primary function of which is to supplement the pleadings for the purpose of disclosing the real points of dispute between the parties and affording an adequate factual basis during the preparation for trial. The liberty of a party to avail itself of this procedure, as an attribute of discovery, is "well-nigh unrestricted if the matters inquired into are otherwise relevant and not privileged, and the inquiry is made in good faith and within the bounds of the law." (*GR 155010, 16 Aug 04*)

Credible evidence

It is a legal truism that evidence, to be believed, must not only proceed from the mouth of a credible witness, but must be credible in itself. (*GR 137288, 11 Dec 01*)

As further laid down in *GR 137288*—

We have no test of the truth of human testimony, except in conformity with our knowledge, observation, and experience and whatever is repugnant to these belongs to the miraculous and is outside of judicial cognizance.

Well-settled is the rule that the findings of facts and assessment of credibility of witnesses is a matter best left to the trial court because of its unique position of having observed that elusive and incommunicable evidence of the witnesses' deportment on the stand while testifying, which opportunity is denied to the appellate courts. Only the trial judge can observe the furtive glance, blush of conscious shame, hesitation, flippant or sneering tone, calmness, sigh, or the scant or full realization of an oath – all of which are useful aids for an accurate determination of a witness' honesty and sincerity. The trial court's findings are accorded finality, unless there appears in the record some fact or circumstance of weight which the lower court may have overlooked, misunderstood or misappreciated, and which, if properly considered, would alter the result of the case. (*GR 131915, 3 Sep 03*)

The rationale for this doctrine is that—

The trial judge is able to detect that sometimes thin line between fact and prevarication that will determine the guilt and innocence of the accused. That line may not be discernible from a mere reading of the impersonal record by the reviewing court. The record will not reveal those tell-tale signs that will affirm the truth or expose the contrivance, like the angry flush of an insistent assertion; or the sudden pallor of a discovered lie; or the tremulous mutter of a reluctant answer; or the forthright tone of a ready reply. The record will not show if the eyes have darted in evasion, or looked down in confession, or gazed steadily with a serenity that has nothing to distort or conceal. The record will not show if tears were shed in anger, or in shame, or in remembered pain, or in feigned innocence. Only the judge trying the case can see all these and on the basis of his observations arrive at an informed and reasoned verdict.

In criminal jurisprudence, when the issue is one of credibility of witnesses, appellate courts will not disturb the findings of the trial court and the Court will respect these findings considering that the trial court is in a better position to decide the question, having heard the witnesses themselves and observed their deportment and manner of testifying during the trial. Of course, the rule admits of certain exceptions: (a) when patent inconsistencies in the statement of witnesses are ignored by the trial court, or (b) when the conclusions arrived at are clearly unsupported by the evidence. (*GR 128890, 31 May 00*)

Settled is the rule that the factual findings of the trial court, especially on the credibility of witnesses are accorded great weight and respect. This is so because the trial court has the advantage of observing the witnesses through the different indicators of truthfulness or falsehood, such as the angry flush of an insisted assertion, the sudden pallor of a discovered lie, the tremulous mutter of a reluctant answer, or the forthright tone of a ready reply; or the furtive glance, the blush of conscious shame, the hesitation, the sincere or the flippant sneering tone, the heat, the calmness, the yawn, the sigh, the candor or lack of it, the scant or full realization of the solemnity of an oath, the carriage and mien. (*GR 127803, 28 Aug 00*)

A few discrepancies and inconsistencies in the testimonies of witnesses referring to minor details do not impair their credibility. Minor inconsistencies even tend to strengthen the credibility of a witness because they discount the possibility that the testimony was rehearsed. As regards the actuations of the witnesses at the time of the incident, it is settled that there is simply no standard form of behavioral response that can be expected from anyone when confronted with a strange, startling, or frightful occurrence. (*GR 174775, 11 Oct 07*)

DNA Evidence

DNA is the fundamental building block of a person's entire genetic make-up. DNA is found in all human cells and is the same in every cell of the same person. Genetic identity is unique. Hence, a person's DNA profile can determine his identity. (*GR 171713, 17 Dec 07*). DNA analysis is a procedure in which DNA extracted from a biological sample obtained from an individual is examined. The DNA is processed to generate a pattern, or a DNA profile, for the individual from whom the sample is taken. This DNA profile is unique for each person, except for identical twins. (*Ibid.*)

Thus—

Everyone is born with a distinct genetic blueprint called DNA (deoxyribonucleic acid). It is exclusive to an individual (except in the rare occurrence of identical twins that share a single, fertilized egg), and DNA is unchanging throughout life. Being a component of every cell in the human body, the DNA of an individual's blood is the very DNA in his or her skin cells, hair follicles, muscles, semen, samples from buccal swabs, saliva, or other body parts.

The chemical structure of DNA has four bases. They are known as A (Adenine), G (guanine), C (cystosine) and T (thymine). The order in which the four bases appear in an individual's DNA determines his or her physical make up. And since DNA is a double stranded molecule, it is composed of two specific paired bases, A-T or T-A and G-C or C-G. These are called "genes."

Every *gene* has a certain number of the above base pairs distributed in a particular sequence. This gives a person his or her genetic code. Somewhere in the DNA framework, nonetheless, are sections that differ.

They are known as "*polymorphic loci,*" which are the areas analyzed in DNA typing (profiling, tests, fingerprinting). In other words, DNA typing simply means determining the "*polymorphic loci.*"

How is DNA typing performed? From a DNA sample obtained or extracted, a molecular biologist may proceed to analyze it in several ways. There are five (5) techniques to conduct DNA typing. They are: the *RFLP* (*restriction fragment length polymorphism*); "*reverse dot blot*" or HLA DQ a/Pm loci which was used in 287 cases that were admitted as evidence by 37 courts in the U.S. as of November 1994; DNA process; VNTR (variable number tandem repeats); and the most recent which is known as the PCR-([polymerase] chain reaction) based STR (short tandem repeats) method which, as of 1996, was availed of by most forensic laboratories in the world. PCR is the process of replicating or copying DNA in an evidence sample a million times through repeated cycling of a reaction involving the so-called DNA polymerize enzyme. *STR,* on the other hand, takes measurements in 13 separate places and can match two (2) samples with a reported theoretical error rate of less than one (1) in a trillion.

Just like in fingerprint analysis, in DNA typing, "*matches*" are determined. To illustrate, when DNA or fingerprint tests are done to identify a suspect in a criminal case, the evidence collected from the crime scene is compared with the "*known*" print. If a substantial amount of the identifying features are the same, the DNA or fingerprint is deemed to be a match. But then, even if only one feature of the DNA or fingerprint is different, it is deemed not to have come from the suspect.

As earlier stated, certain regions of human DNA show variations between people. In each of these regions, a person possesses two genetic types called *"allele,"* one inherited from each parent. In [a] paternity test, the forensic scientist looks at a number of these variable regions in an individual to produce a DNA profile. Comparing next the DNA profiles of the mother and child, it is possible to determine which half of the child's DNA was inherited from the mother. The other half must have been inherited from the biological father. The alleged father's profile is then examined to ascertain whether he has the DNA types in his profile, which match the paternal types in the child. If the man's DNA types do not match that of the child, the man is excluded as the father. If the DNA types match, then he is not excluded as the father.

In the newly promulgated rules on DNA evidence it is provided:

SEC. 3 *Definition of Terms.* – For purposes of this Rule, the following terms shall be defined as follows:

x x x x

(c)   "DNA evidence" constitutes the totality of the DNA profiles, results and other genetic information directly generated from DNA testing of biological samples;

(d)   "DNA profile" means genetic information derived from DNA testing of a biological sample obtained from a person, which biological sample is clearly identifiable as originating from that person;

(e)   "DNA testing" means verified and credible scientific methods which include the extraction of DNA from biological samples, the generation of DNA profiles and the comparison of the information obtained from the DNA testing of biological samples for the purpose of determining, with reasonable certainty, whether or not the DNA obtained from two or more distinct biological samples originates from the same person (direct identification) or if the biological samples originate from related persons (kinship analysis); and

(f)   "Probability of Parentage" means the numerical estimate for the likelihood of parentage of a putative parent compared with the probability of a random match of two unrelated individuals in a given population.

DNA analysis may provide the definitive key to the resolution of the issue of support, Philippine Supreme Court thus said:

Our faith in DNA testing, however, was not quite so steadfast in the previous decade. In *Pe Lim v. Court of Appeals* (336 Phil. 741, 270 SCRA 1), promulgated in 1997, we cautioned against the use of DNA because "DNA, being a relatively new science, (had) not as yet been accorded official recognition by our courts. Paternity (would) still have to be resolved by such conventional evidence as the relevant incriminating acts,verbal and written, by the putative father."

In 2001, however, we opened the possibility of admitting DNA as evidence of parentage, as enunciated in *Tijing v. Court of Appeals* [G.R. No. 125901, 8 March 2001, 354 SCRA 17] x x x

Parentage will still be resolved using conventional methods unless we adopt the modern and scientific ways available. Fortunately, we have now the facility and expertise in using DNA test for identification and parentage testing. The University of the Philippines Natural Science Research Institute (UP-NSRI) DNA Analysis Laboratory has now the capability to conduct DNA typing using short tandem repeat (STR) analysis. The analysis is based on the fact that the DNA of a child/person has two (2) copies, one copy from the mother and the other from the father. The DNA from the mother, the alleged father and child are analyzed to establish parentage. Of course, being a novel scientific technique, the use of DNA test as evidence is still open to challenge. Eventually, as the appropriate case comes, courts should not hesitate to rule on the admissibility of DNA evidence. For it was said, that courts should apply the results of science when competently obtained in aid of situations presented, since to reject said results is to deny progress. x x x

The New Rules on DNA Evidence allows the conduct of DNA testing, either *motu proprio* or upon application of any person who has a legal interest in the matter in litigation, thus:

SEC. 4. *Application for DNA Testing Order.* – The appropriate court may, at any time, either *motu proprio* or on application of any person who has a legal interest in the matter in litigation, order a DNA testing. Such order shall issue after due hearing and notice to the parties upon a showing of the following:

(a) A biological sample exists that is relevant to the cas

(b) The biological sample: (i) was not previously subjected to the type of DNA testing now requested; or (ii) was previously subjected to DNA testing, but the results may require confirmation for good reasons;

(c) The DNA testing uses a scientifically valid technique;

(d) The DNA testing has the scientific potential to produce new information that is relevant to the proper resolution of the case; and

(e) The existence of other factors, if any, which the court may consider as potentially affecting the accuracy or integrity of the DNA testing.

As defined above, the term "biological sample" means any organic material originating from a person's body, even if found in inanimate objects, that is susceptible to DNA testing. This includes blood, saliva, and other body fluids, tissues, hairs and bones.

When a crime is committed, material is collected from the scene of the crime or from the victim's body for the suspect's DNA. This is the evidence sample. The evidence sample is then matched with the reference sample taken from the suspect and the victim. (*GR 144656, 9 May 02*)

The purpose of DNA testing is to ascertain whether an association exists between the evidence sample and the reference sample. The samples collected are subjected to various chemical processes to establish their profile. The test may yield three possible results:

174

(1) The samples are different and therefore must have originated from different sources (exclusion). This conclusion is absolute and requires no further analysis or discussion;

(2) It is not possible to be sure, based on the results of the test, whether the samples have similar DNA types (inconclusive). This might occur for a variety of reasons including degradation, contamination, or failure of some aspect of the protocol. Various parts of the analysis might then be repeated with the same or a different sample, to obtain a more conclusive result; or

(3) The samples are similar, and could have originated from the same source (inclusion). In such a case, the samples are found to be similar, the analyst proceeds to determine the statistical significance of the Similarity.

In assessing the probative value of DNA evidence, therefore, courts should consider, among others things, the following data: how the samples were collected, how they were handled, the possibility of contamination of the samples, the procedure followed in analyzing the samples, whether the proper standards and procedures were followed in conducting the tests, and the qualification of the analyst who conducted the tests. (*Ibid.*)

After the DNA analysis is obtained, it shall be incumbent upon the parties who wish to avail of the same to offer the results in accordance with the rules of evidence. The RTC, in evaluating the DNA results upon presentation, shall assess the same as evidence in keeping with Sections 7 and 8 of the Rules, to wit:

SEC. 7. *Assessment of probative value of DNA evidence.* – In assessing the probative value of the DNA evidence presented, the court shall consider the following:

(a) The chain of custody, including how the biological samples were collected, how they were handled, and the possibility of contamination of the samples;

(b) The DNA testing methodology, including the procedure followed in analyzing the samples, the advantages and disadvantages of the procedure, and compliance with the scientifically valid standards in conducting the tests;

(c) The forensic DNA laboratory, including accreditation by any reputable standards-setting institution and the qualification of the analyst who conducted the tests. If the laboratory is not accredited, the relevant experience of the laboratory in forensic casework and credibility shall be properly established; and

(d) The reliability of the testing result, as hereinafter provided.

SEC. 8. *Reliability of DNA testing methodology.*–In evaluating whether the DNA testing methodology is reliable, the court shall consider the following:

(a) The falsifiability of the principles or methods used, that is, whether the theory or technique can be and has been tested;

(b) The subjection to peer review and publication of the principles or methods;

(c) The general acceptance of the principles or methods by the relevant scientific community;

(d) The existence and maintenance of standards and controls to ensure the correctness of data gathered;

(e) The existence of an appropriate reference population database; and

(f) The general degree of confidence attributed to mathematical calculations used in comparing DNA profiles and the significance and limitation of statistical calculations used in comparing DNA profiles.

Electronic Evidence

Republic Act No. 8792, otherwise known in the Philippines as the Electronic Commerce Act of 2000, considers an electronic data message or an electronic document as the functional equivalent of a written document for evidentiary purposes. The Rules on Electronic Evidence regards an electronic document as admissible in evidence if it complies with the rules on admissibility prescribed by the Rules of Court and related laws, and is authenticated in the manner prescribed by the said Rules. An electronic document is also the equivalent of an original document under the Best Evidence Rule, if it is a printout or output readable by sight or other means, shown to reflect the data accurately. (*GR 170633, 17 Oct 07*)

Thus, to be admissible in evidence as an electronic data message or to be considered as the functional equivalent of an original document under the Best

Evidence Rule, *the writing must foremost be an "electronic data message" or an "electronic document." (Ibid.)*

The Electronic Commerce Act of 2000 defines electronic data message and electronic document as follows:

Sec. 5. ***Definition of Terms.*** For the purposes of this Act, the following terms are defined, as follows: xxx

c. "Electronic Data Message" refers to information generated, sent, received or stored by electronic, optical or similar means. xxx

f. "Electronic Document" refers to information or the representation of information, data, figures, symbols or other modes of written expression, described or however represented, by which a right is established or an obligation extinguished, or by which a fact may be proved and affirmed, which is received, recorded, transmitted, stored, processed, retrieved or produced electronically.

The Implementing Rules and Regulations (IRR) of R.A. No. 8792, which was signed on July 13, 2000 defines the terms as:

Sec. 6. ***Definition of Terms.*** For the purposes of this Act and these Rules, the following terms are defined, as follows: x x x

(e) "Electronic Data Message" refers to information generated, sent, received or stored by electronic, optical or similar means, *but not limited to, electronic data interchange (EDI), electronic mail, telegram, telex or telecopy. Throughout these Rules, the term "electronic data message" shall be equivalent to and be used interchangeably with "electronic document."* x x x

(h) "Electronic Document" refers to information or the representation of information, data, figures, symbols or other modes of written expression, described or however represented, by which a right is established or an obligation extinguished, or by which a fact may be proved and affirmed, which is received, recorded, transmitted, stored, processed, retrieved or produced electronically. *Throughout these Rules, the term "electronic document" shall be equivalent to and be used interchangeably with "electronic data message."*

As *GR 170633(supra)* further states:

The phrase *"but not limited to, electronic data interchange (EDI), electronic mail, telegram, telex or telecopy"* in the IRR's definition of "electronic data message" is copied from the Model Law on Electronic Commerce adopted by the United Nations Commission on International Trade Law (UNCITRAL), from which majority of the provisions of R.A. No. 8792 were taken. While Congress deleted this phrase in the Electronic Commerce Act of 2000, the drafters of the IRR reinstated it.

The deletion by Congress of the said phrase is significant and pivotal, as discussed hereunder.

The clause on the interchangeability of the terms "electronic data message" and "electronic document" was the result of the Senate of the Philippines' adoption, in Senate Bill 1902, of the phrase "electronic data message" and the House of Representative's employment, in House Bill 9971, of the term "electronic document." In order to expedite the reconciliation of the two versions, the technical working group of the Bicameral Conference Committee adopted both terms and intended them to be the equivalent of each one. Be that as it may, there is a slight difference between the two terms. While "data message" has reference to *information electronically sent, stored or transmitted, it does not necessarily mean that it will give rise to a right or extinguish an obligation,* unlike an electronic document. Evident from the law, however, is the legislative intent to give the two terms the same construction.

The Rules on Electronic Evidence promulgated by the Philippine Court defines the said terms in the following manner:

SECTION 1. *Definition of Terms.* – For purposes of these Rules, the following terms are defined, as follows: x x x

(g) "Electronic data message" refers to information generated, sent, received or stored by electronic, optical or similar means.

(h)   "

Electronic document" refers to information or the representation of information, data, figures, symbols or other modes of written expression, described or however represented, by which a right is established or an obligation extinguished, or by which a fact may be proved and affirmed, which is received, recorded, transmitted, stored, processed, retrieved or produced electronically. *It includes digitally signed documents and print-out or output, readable by sight or other means, which accurately reflects the electronic data message or electronic document. For purposes of these Rules, the term "electronic document" may be used interchangeably with "electronic data message."*

As the ruling further states:

Given these definitions, we go back to the original question: Is an original printout of a *facsimile transmission* an electronic data message or electronic document?

The definitions under the Electronic Commerce Act of 2000, its IRR and the Rules on Electronic Evidence, *at first glance*, convey the impression that *facsimile_transmissions* are electronic data messages or electronic documents because they are *sent by electronic means*. The expanded definition of an "electronic data message" under the IRR, consistent with the UNCITRAL Model Law, further supports this theory considering that the enumeration "xxx [is] not limited to, electronic data interchange (EDI), electronic mail, telegram, telex or *telecopy*." And to telecopy is *to send a document from one place to another via a fax machine*.

As further guide for the Court in its task of statutory construction, Section 37 of the Electronic Commerce Act of 2000 provides that--

Unless otherwise expressly provided for, the interpretation of this Act *shall give due regard to its international origin* and the need to promote uniformity in its application and the observance of good faith in international trade relations. The generally accepted principles of international law and convention on electronic commerce shall likewise be considered.

Obviously, the "international origin" mentioned in this section can only refer to the UNCITRAL Model Law, and the UNCITRAL's definition of "data message":

"Data message" means information generated, sent, received or stored by electronic, optical or similar means *including, but not limited to, electronic data interchange (EDI), electronic mail, telegram, telex or telecopy.*

is substantially the same as the IRR's characterization of an "electronic data message."

However, Congress deleted the phrase, *"but not limited to, electronic data interchange (EDI), electronic mail, telegram, telex or telecopy,"* and replaced the term "data message" (as found in the UNCITRAL Model Law) with "electronic data message." This legislative divergence from what is assumed as the term's "international origin" has bred uncertainty and now impels the Court to make an inquiry into the true intent of the framers of the law. Indeed, in the construction or interpretation of a legislative measure, the primary rule is to search for and determine the intent and spirit of the law. A construction should be rejected that gives to the language used in a statute a meaning that does not accomplish the purpose for which the statute was enacted, and that tends to defeat the ends which are sought to be attained by the enactment.

Interestingly, when Senator Ramon B. Magsaysay, Jr., the principal author of Senate Bill 1902 (the predecessor of R.A. No. 8792), sponsored the bill on second reading, he proposed to adopt the term "data message" as formulated and defined in the

182

UNCITRAL Model Law. During the period of amendments, however, the term evolved into *"electronic* data message," and the phrase *"but not limited to, electronic data interchange (EDI), electronic mail, telegram, telex or telecopy"* in the UNCITRAL Model Law was deleted. Furthermore, the term "electronic data message," though maintaining its description under the UNCITRAL Model Law, except for the aforesaid deleted phrase, *conveyed a different meaning*, as revealed in the following proceedings x x x

Senator Santiago. Yes, Mr. President. I will furnish a copy together with the explanation of this proposed amendment.

And then finally, before I leave the Floor, may I please be allowed to go back to Section 5; the Definition of Terms. In light of the acceptance by the good Senator of my proposed amendments, it will then become necessary to add certain terms in our list of terms to be defined. I would like to add a definition on what is "data," what is "electronic record" and what is an "electronic record system."

If the gentleman will give me permission, I will proceed with the proposed amendment on Definition of Terms, Section 5.

Senator Magsaysay. Please go ahead, Senator Santiago.

Senator Santiago. We are in Part 1, short title on the Declaration of Policy, Section 5, Definition of Terms.

At the appropriate places in the listing of these terms that have to be defined since these are arranged alphabetically, Mr. President, I would like to insert the term DATA and its definition. So, the amendment will read: "DATA" MEANS REPRESENTATION, IN ANY FORM, OF INFORMATION OR CONCEPTS.

The explanation is this: This definition of "data" or "data" as it is now fashionably pronounced in America - - the definition of "data" ensures that our bill applies to any form of information in an electronic record, whether these are figures, facts or ideas.

So again, the proposed amendment is this: "DATA" MEANS REPRESENTATIONS, IN ANY FORM, OF INFORMATION OR CONCEPTS.

Senator Magsaysay. May I know how will this affect the definition of "Data Message" which encompasses electronic records, electronic writings and electronic documents?

Senator Santiago. These are completely congruent with each other. These are compatible. When we define "data," we are simply reinforcing the definition of what is a data message.

Senator Magsaysay. It is accepted, Mr. President.

Senator Santiago. Thank you. The next term is "ELECTRONIC RECORD." The proposed amendment is as follows:

"ELECTRONIC RECORD" MEANS DATA THAT IS RECORDED OR STORED ON ANY MEDIUM IN OR BY A COMPUTER SYSTEM OR OTHER SIMILAR DEVICE, THAT CAN BE READ OR PERCEIVED BY A PERSON OR A COMPUTER SYSTEM OR OTHER SIMILAR

DEVICE. IT INCLUDES A DISPLAY, PRINTOUT OR OTHER OUTPUT OF THAT DATA.

The explanation for this term and its definition is as follows: The term "ELECTRONIC RECORD" fixes the scope of our bill. The record is the data. The record may be on any medium. It is electronic because it is recorded or stored in or by a computer system or a similar device.

The amendment is intended to apply, for example, to data on magnetic strips on cards or in Smart cards. *As drafted, it would not apply to telexes or faxes, except computer-generated faxes, unlike the United Nations model law on electronic commerce. It would also not apply to regular digital telephone conversations since the information is not recorded. It would apply to voice mail since the information has been recorded in or by a device similar to a computer. Likewise, video records are not covered. Though when the video is transferred to a website, it would be covered because of the involvement of the computer. Music recorded by a computer system on a compact disc would be covered.*

In short, not all data recorded or stored in digital form is covered. A computer or a similar device has to be involved in its creation or storage. The term "similar device" does not extend to all devices that create or store data in digital form. Although things that are not recorded or preserved by or in a computer system are omitted from this bill, these may well be admissible under other rules of law. This provision focuses on replacing the search for originality proving the reliability of systems instead of that of individual records and using standards to show systems reliability.

Paper records that are produced directly by a computer system such as printouts are themselves electronic records being just the means of intelligible display of the contents of the record. Photocopies of the printout would be paper record subject to the usual rules about copies, but the original printout would be subject to the rules of admissibility of this bill.

However, printouts that are used only as paper records and whose computer origin is never again called on are treated as paper records. In that case, the reliability of the computer system that produces the record is irrelevant to its reliability.

Senator Magsaysay. Mr. President, if my memory does not fail me, earlier, the lady Senator accepted that we use the term "Data Message" rather than "ELECTRONIC RECORD" in being consistent with the UNCITRAL term of "Data Message." *So with the new amendment of defining "ELECTRONIC RECORD," will this affect her accepting of the use of "Data Message" instead of "ELECTRONIC RECORD"?*

Senator Santiago. No, it will not. Thank you for reminding me. *The term I would like to insert is ELECTRONIC DATA MESSAGE in lieu of "ELECTRONIC RECORD."*

Senator Magsaysay. *Then we are, in effect,* **amending the term of the definition of "Data Message" on page 2A, line 31, to which we have no objection.**

Senator Santiago. Thank you, Mr. President. x x x
x

Senator Santiago. Mr. President, I have proposed all the amendments that I desire to, including the amendment on the effect of error or change. I will provide the language of the amendment together with the explanation supporting that amendment to the distinguished sponsor and then he can feel free to take it up in any session without any further intervention.

Senator Magsaysay. Before we end, Mr. President, I understand from the proponent of these amendments that these are based on the *Canadian E-commerce Law of 1998*. Is that not right?

Senator Santiago. *That is correct.*

Thus, when the Senate consequently voted to adopt the term "electronic data message," it was consonant with the explanation of Senator Miriam Defensor-Santiago that it would not apply *"to telexes or faxes, except computer-generated faxes, unlike the United Nations model law on electronic commerce."* In explaining the term "electronic record" patterned after the E-Commerce Law of Canada, Senator Defensor-Santiago had in mind the term "electronic data message." This term then, while maintaining part of the UNCITRAL Model Law's terminology of "data message," has assumed a different context, this time, consonant with the term "electronic record" in the law of Canada. It accounts for the addition of the word "electronic" and the deletion of the phrase *"but not limited to, electronic data interchange (EDI), electronic mail, telegram, telex or telecopy."* Noteworthy is that the Uniform Law Conference of

Canada, explains the term "electronic record," as drafted in the Uniform Electronic Evidence Act, in a manner strikingly similar to Sen. Santiago's explanation during the Senate deliberations:

"Electronic record" fixes the scope of the Act. The record is the data. The record may be any medium. It is "electronic" because it is recorded or stored in or by a computer system or similar device. The Act is intended to apply, for example, to data on magnetic strips on cards, or in smart cards. As drafted, *it would not apply to telexes or faxes (except computer-generated faxes), unlike the United Nations Model Law on Electronic Commerce.* It would also not apply to regular digital telephone conversations, since the information is not recorded. It would apply to voice mail, since the information has been recorded in or by a device similar to a computer. Likewise video records are not covered, though when the video is transferred to a Web site it would be, because of the involvement of the computer. Music recorded by a computer system on a compact disk would be covered.

In short, not all data recorded or stored in "digital" form is covered. A computer or similar device has to be involved in its creation or storage. The term "similar device" does not extend to all devices that create or store data in digital form. Although things that are not recorded or preserved by or in a computer system are omitted from this Act, they may well be admissible under other rules of law. This Act focuses on replacing the search for originality, proving the reliability of systems instead of that of individual records, and using standards to show systems reliability.

Paper records that are produced directly by a computer system, such as printouts, are themselves electronic records, being just the means of intelligible display of the contents of the record. Photocopies of the printout would be paper records subject to the usual rules about copies, but the "original" printout would be subject to the rules of admissibility of this Act. However, printouts that are used only as paper records, and whose computer origin is never again called on, are treated as paper records. See subsection 4(2). In this case the reliability of the computer system that produced the record is relevant to its reliability.

There is no question then that when Congress formulated the term "electronic data message," it intended the same meaning as the term "electronic record" in the Canada law. This construction of the term "electronic data message," which *excludes telexes or faxes, except computer-generated faxes*, is in harmony with the Electronic Commerce Law's focus on "paperless" communications and the "functional equivalent approach" that it espouses. In fact, the deliberations of the Legislature are replete with discussions on paperless and digital transactions.

Facsimile transmissions are not, in this sense, "paperless," but verily are paper-based.

A facsimile machine, which was first patented in 1843 by Alexander Bain, is a device that can send or receive pictures and text over a telephone line. It works by digitizing an image—dividing it into a grid of dots. Each dot is either on or off, depending on whether it is black or white. Electronically, each dot is represented by a bit that has a value of either 0 (off) or 1 (on). In this way, the fax machine translates a picture into a series of zeros and ones (called a bit map) that can be transmitted like normal computer data. On the receiving side, a fax machine reads the incoming data, translates the zeros and ones back into dots, and reprints the picture. A fax machine is essentially an image scanner, a modem and a computer printer combined into a highly specialized package. The scanner converts the content of a physical document into a digital image, the modem sends the image data over a phone line, and the printer at the other end makes a duplicate of the original document. Thus, in *Garvida v. Sales, Jr.*, where we explained the unacceptability of filing pleadings through fax machines, we ruled that:

A facsimile or fax transmission is a process involving the transmission and reproduction of printed and graphic matter by scanning an original copy, one elemental area at a time, and representing the shade or tone of each area by a specified amount of electric current. The current is transmitted as a signal over regular telephone lines or via microwave relay and is used by the receiver to reproduce an image of the elemental area in the proper position and the correct shade. The receiver is equipped with a stylus or other device that produces a printed record on paper referred to as a facsimile.

x x x A facsimile is not a genuine and authentic pleading. It is, at best, an exact copy preserving all the marks of an original. Without the original, there is no way of determining on its face whether the facsimile pleading is genuine and authentic and was originally signed by the party and his counsel. It may, in fact, be a sham pleading.

Accordingly, in an ordinary facsimile transmission, there exists an original *paper-based* information or data that is scanned, sent through a phone line, and re-printed at the receiving end. Be it noted that in enacting the Electronic Commerce Act of 2000, Congress intended *virtual or paperless* writings to be the *functional* equivalent and to have the same *legal function* as paper-based documents. Further, in a virtual or paperless environment, technically, there is no original copy to speak of, as all direct printouts of the virtual reality are the same, in all respects, and are considered as originals. Ineluctably, the law's definition of "electronic data message," which, as aforesaid, is interchangeable with "electronic document," could not have included *facsimile transmissions*, which have an *original paper-based* copy *as sent* and a *paper-based facsimile* copy *as received*. These two copies are distinct from each other, and have different legal effects. While Congress anticipated future developments in communications and computer technology when it drafted the law, it excluded the early forms of technology, like telegraph, telex and telecopy (except computer-generated faxes, which is a newer development as compared to the ordinary fax machine to fax machine transmission), when it defined the term "electronic data message."

Clearly then, the IRR went beyond the parameters of the law when it adopted verbatim the UNCITRAL Model Law's definition of "data message," without considering the intention of Congress when the latter deleted the phrase *"but not limited to, electronic data interchange (EDI), electronic mail, telegram, telex or telecopy."* The inclusion of this phrase in the IRR offends a basic tenet in the exercise of the rule-making power of administrative agencies. After all, the power of administrative officials to promulgate rules in the implementation of a statute is necessarily limited to what is found in the legislative enactment itself. The implementing rules and regulations of a law cannot extend the law or expand its coverage, as the power to amend or repeal a statute is vested in the Legislature. Thus, if a discrepancy occurs between the basic law and an implementing rule or regulation, it is the former that prevails, because the law cannot be broadened by a mere administrative issuance— an administrative agency certainly cannot amend an act of Congress. Had the Legislature really wanted ordinary fax transmissions to be covered by the mantle of the Electronic Commerce Act of 2000, it could have easily lifted without a bit of tatter the entire wordings of the UNCITRAL Model Law.

Incidentally, the National Statistical Coordination Board Task Force on the Measurement of E-Commerce, on November 22, 2006, recommended a working definition of "electronic commerce," as "[a]ny commercial transaction conducted through electronic, optical and similar medium, mode, instrumentality and technology. The transaction includes the sale or purchase of goods and services, between individuals, households, businesses and governments conducted over computer-mediated networks through the Internet, mobile phones, electronic data interchange (EDI) and other channels through open and closed networks." The Task Force's proposed definition is similar to the Organization of Economic Cooperation and Development's (OECD's) broad definition as it covers transactions made over any network, and, in addition, it adopted the following provisions of the OECD definition: (1) for transactions, it covers sale or purchase of goods and services; (2) for channel/network, it considers any computer-mediated network and NOT limited to Internet alone; (3) it excludes transactions received/placed using *fax*, telephone or non-interactive mail; (4) it considers payments done online or offline; and (5) it considers delivery made online (like downloading of purchased books, music or software programs) or offline (deliveries of goods).

We, therefore, conclude that the terms "electronic data message" and "electronic document," as defined under the Electronic Commerce Act of 2000, do not include a facsimile transmission. Accordingly, a facsimile transmission cannot be considered as electronic evidence. It is not the functional equivalent of an original under the Best Evidence Rule and is not admissible as electronic evidence.

Since a facsimile transmission is not an "electronic data message" or an "electronic document," and cannot be considered as electronic evidence by the Court, with greater reason is a photocopy of such a fax transmission not electronic evidence. In the present case, therefore, *Pro Forma* Invoice Nos. **ST2-POSTS0401-1** and **ST2-POSTS0401-2** (Exhibits "E" and "F"), which are **mere photocopies** of the original fax transmittals, are not electronic evidence, contrary to the position of both the trial and the appellate courts.

Polygraph test

A polygraph is an electromechanical instrument that simultaneously measures and records certain physiological changes in the human body that are believed to be involuntarily caused by an examinee's conscious attempt to deceive the questioner. The theory behind a polygraph or lie detector test is that a person who lies deliberately will have a rising blood pressure and a subconscious block in breathing, which will be recorded on the graph. However, American courts almost uniformly reject the results of polygraph tests when offered in evidence for the purpose of establishing the guilt or innocence of one accused of a crime, whether the accused or the prosecution seeks its introduction, for the reason that polygraph has not as yet attained scientific acceptance as a reliable and accurate means of ascertaining truth or deception. (*GR 116196-97, 23 Jun 99*)

Paraffin Test

Scientific experts concur in the view that the paraffin test has proved extremely unreliable in use. The only thing that it can definitely establish is the presence or absence of nitrates or nitrites on the hand. It cannot be established from this test alone that the source pf the nitrates or nitrites was the discharge of firearm. The person may have handled one or more of a number of substances which give the same positive reaction for nitrates or nitrites, such as explosives, fireworks, fertilizers, Pharmaceuticals and leguminous plants such as peas, beans and alfalta. A person who uses tobacco may also have nitrate or nitrite deposits on his hands since these substances are present in the products of combustion of tobacco. The presence of nitrates should be taken only as an indication of a possibility or even of a probability but not of infallibility that a person has fired a gun, since nitrates are also admittedly found in substances other than gunpowder. (*GR 116730, 16 Nov 95*; see Criminalities, Bankcroft Whitney Co., 1915 ed., p. 141; Richardson, Modern Scientific Evidence, Anderson Co., p. 495 cited in *People vs. Teehankee, Jr.*, G.R. No. 111206-08, October 6, 1995)

For more information on Narma Books,
visit **Facebook** and click on
www.facebook.com and search for:
Narma Books.
We are on Twitter, too.
Follow us—
www.twitter.com/narmabooks.
View us on Pinterest—
www.pinterest.com/narmabooks.
Find us on Scribd—
www.scribd.com/narmabooks.
Read our inspirational shares and selections:
Click on—
http://nrcsinspirational.wordpress.com.
Or, see us on
Google Plus—
Narma Books
and
nrcsinspirational
*****

Other works

Other works from Narma Books include fiction dealing with the Mideast, such as:

The Last Traces of Hope is now available both as print and e-book. It is a novel about the Mideast turmoil and how it affected the lives of those who were trapped in the 1990 Iraqi invasion of Kuwait. A ship manned by Filipino crew members was docked in the international port of Kuwait on August 2, 1990 when the incursion transpired. This book tells what happened when the vessel was about to sail and after it did.

The novel is available in print at **www.createspace.com/3621484** and as an e-book at **www.smashwords.com**. It is also available in Kindle version at **https://kdp.amazon.com.**

"Harvest of Sand" tells us of a turmoil in the Middle East and how foreign lives were affected. It is an account of events which transpired in the Middle East in 1990 spawned by Iraq's incursion into Kuwait. On August 2, 1990 in Kuwait City, it was getting late but Brian Rios, a deputy employment and welfare attaché assigned at the Philippine Embassy there, knew he was facing a sleepless night. More people would be arriving and would be joining the multitude of those who were already jostled in the embassy premises. The succeeding scenes were unnerving.

The story is included in the author's collection of his other works of fiction, *"Fiction Assemblage,"* made up of a novella and four short stories which are available either in print or in e-book format.

The collection may be procured online through— *https://www.createspace.com/3598890*.

More Books from the Author:

Fiction

* **A Man and A Girl**

 - Available as one of the collected stories in Fiction Assemblage

* **An Awakening and Losing**

 - Available at: **www.createspace.com/3565490**

* **Menace on the Face of the Red Moon**

 - Available at: **www.createspace.com/3571177**

Non-fiction

o **Crime, Retribution and Exoneration**

 - Available at: **www.createspace.com/3697327**

Inspirational:

-- Finding Pathways through the Community
- Available in print and as an e-book:
www.createspace.com/3747127

AUTHOR'S NOTE

This book is a work of fiction and represents the dilemma that Mideast transients have to contend with in living life in that land. The characters created herein are purely fictional and any similarity or resemblance to actual persons is purely coincidental. The places described, however, are real and the events that transpire forming as backdrop of the story may have actually happened. Inclusion of aspects thereof is imperative to give flavor to the story.

The author is motivated solely by a desire to provide entertainment to the readers, and no offense, if any, is intended to an individual or group, be it as to their beliefs or well-being.

ACKNOWLEDGMENT

The author acknowledges the invaluable help and assistance he obtained from various sectors in the preparation of this book and his other works previously published as well as those still being prepared for publication.

His appreciation goes to those who shared with him their full support and positive stance as well as their kind indulgence as the author gropes along the pathways to self-publication.

Such regard likewise extends to the members of his family, peers and friends who in one way or another have taken part in making this venture a success.

The author is furthermore indebted to his readers for their patronage of his works and staying with him in the journey through pages of the printed word.

ABOUT THE AUTHOR

The author, 62 years of age, resides in the Philippines, where he is a member of the *Sumakwelan*, an organization of vernacular writers from the Western Visayan region and portions of Mindanao Island in the Philippines.

His works include several titles in non-fiction and some in fiction and poetry. He has been engaged in vernacular writing in his country since he was a teenager. He is currently working on the translation of his literary works into the English language. He assures his readers, however, of his earnest efforts in seeing to it that nothing is missed in the course of the translation.

The author has taught Remedial Law at Aklan College, Kalibo, Aklan, Philippines and has been engaged in the advocacy of law in the Philippines.

He may be reached at this e-mail address— nrcsbookshop@ymail.com.

His availability may be had also through:
*www.twitter.com/narmabooks
*www.scribd.com/narmabooks

He may be visited at the following Web sites:
*http://narmabooks.webs.com
*http://nrcsinspirational.wordpress.com
*http://books2narma.wordpress.com

www.ingramcontent.com/pod-product-compliance
Lightning Source LLC
Chambersburg PA
CBHW071425170526
45165CB00001B/402